**More Than A Baseball Team**
**The Saga of the Vancouver Asahi**

By Ted Y. Furumoto and Douglas W. Jackson

Published by Media Tectonics, an imprint of 4M Associates, Inc.

4M Associates Inc.
Daisy Yotsuya 101, 2-9-7 Wakaba,
Shinjuku-ku, Tokyo
160-0011 Japan

isbn 978-4-9906172-0-2 (pbk)
isbn 978-4-9906172-1-0 (ebk)

Cover design by Andrew Pothecary at ForbiddenColour.com
Book design by Joy Mielke

# Contents

Ted Y. Furumoto

# AUTHOR'S PREFACE

I first learned about the Vancouver Asahi when I was a small child.

As did every other boy at that time in Japan, I grew up playing baseball with my friends. I listened to games on the radio, and watched baseball on television with my father. But why would a child living in Japan know about an amateur Nikkei baseball team that disbanded years ago in the far-off foreign land of Canada?

There was a special reason: my father. He had been the Asahi's first ace. Normally a gentleman, quiet and calm in temperament, he became a radically different man when it came to baseball. When watching exhibition games between (losing) Japanese and (winning) American teams, for example, or even when a foreign player on a Japanese team played a role in beating the other Japanese team, my father would get excited, then go into full "baseball rant" as he vented his displeasure and anger.

"What're you doing getting beat like that? We won against stronger players than these!"

My father loved baseball, and could not stop talking when it came to his beloved Vancouver Asahi. There was one thing he was sorry about: that in Japan, their mother country, the number of people who knew about the team was close to zero. The stories my father told me were the stuff of blood and guts, epic sagas that captured my boy's heart.

"We came from behind, and we kept coming from behind," he'd say, or exclaim "And then we shut them out and got the win!" I was so proud of him.

The Vancouver Asahi, who were formed twenty years before the team that became the Yomiuri Giants and later went head to head against them. The Asahi, who made a clean sweep of the leagues on Canada's west coast, and who captured the hearts and minds of every Canadian baseball fan, not just the Nikkei. As the son of Teddy Furumoto, the Asahi's first ace, I too was disappointed, sorry in my own juvenile way that the team was not better known.

My father was only twenty-six years old when he retired from the Asahi as an active player. "You were the ace, couldn't you have played longer?" I asked. My father looked vexed. "My back gave out," he answered abruptly.

He told me how it happened. When the Asahi team was about to conquer the Terminal League for the first time, he took up a defensive position and saved the game with an acrobatic play. He jumped high, twisting in the air while throwing the ball to put the runner out.

"I got pretty good at it," my father would say with quiet pride. It was a speedy, effective, killer move that he made his own. After a while, however, his back could not endure the strain, and he had no choice but to retire.

After Father left the Asahi, he went to study at Michigan State

University. Meanwhile, my grandparents immigrated to Vancouver from Oshimo-gun, in Yamaguchi Prefecture. They ran a rooming house on the outskirts of Japan Town.

My father visited Japan just before the war started. Born and raised in Canada, he stepped onto Japanese soil for only the second time in his life, the first being when he came as part of the Asahi's barnstorming tour of Japan.

Unable to return after the outbreak of war, he was pressed into service as an announcer for NHK's English-language radio broadcasts. He was then dispatched to Singapore and the Philippines as a war correspondent. At the end of the war, he became an interpreter for GHQ (U.S. military headquarters in Japan). He also worked with a major entertainment production company to develop singers and organize big bands for clubs catering to the Occupation forces.

He later worked at the American Embassy, acting as the chief of the translation team for the U.S. Air Force. He also taught English, and afterward became the principal of an English school. While he was at the embassy, he was on a friendly basis with then-Ambassador Reischauer, who invited our family to the embassy Christmas parties.

My father was outgoing and positive, never complaining or displaying any bitterness. However, what gnawed at him was an ongoing disappointment about why a dominant team like the Asahi was not better known in Japan. It was a frustrating dilemma for him, as one of the original Asahi nine and its first ace. Father may have felt that he owed a debt to his fellow players to change this situation.

In 1970 my father flew to Vancouver, returning for the first time in nearly three decades. He was there to hold a memorial service for my grandparents. The last time he had seen them was when he left for Japan before the war.

My grandparents had been sent to different camps. No information is available regarding where. Separated, they died apart from each other. Friendly Nikkei hands must have buried both of them.

Father put up a memorial at the site of the rooming house my grandparents had operated. The memorial was a substitute grave for his parents, who slept somewhere under the vast Canadian earth.

"Return of the Asahi Ace," reported a Canadian newspaper about my father's visit. He received a warm welcome from old fans and surviving players.

Father, who had finally been able to carry out his heart's desire of a memorial service for his parents, passed away at the age of seventy-nine in 1979. What he bequeathed to me was the duty to spread the story of the Vancouver Asahi.

For a long time, though, I was busy leading my own life, and I had no clue about how to expand upon the stories my father told me about the Asahi.

I shall never forget October 2, 1994. I was watching television during dinner. When the Tokyo Broadcasting System affiliate program JNN News Special featuring "The Unknown Canadian Asahi Team" began, I felt as if I were dreaming, and was glued to the screen.

I contacted the producer at once, and he told me about the surviving members of the team, as well as how he had accidentally stumbled upon the team's story during a visit to Canada, and had been inspired to create the program.

I made up my mind to step onto Canadian soil myself. It would be a trip to honor the memories of my father and to visit the country of his birth.

I walked up and down the Powell Street area in Vancouver. I visited the old Powell Street Grounds, which had been renamed Oppenheimer Park. The field was bare and full of small sharp pebbles. There was no lawn, or even weeds, to speak of. It was just an ordinary open space that would have been embarrassing to call a baseball field. But when I stood on home plate and on the pitcher's mound, I could see my father and other young men of the Asahi team playing ball. The images of their glory days filled my mind.

In Toronto, a glorious experience awaited—a reunion of the Vancouver Asahi family. People from all over Canada gathered to greet Teddy Furumoto's son, who had come from Japan. We could not control our tears.

I was impressed with everyone's vitality and energy. The team was the central topic of every conversation. All the stories my father drummed into me paled as I understood for the first time the extraordinary meaning the Asahi held for Japanese-Canadians.

"Even though we are Canadian, never once have we forgotten Japan," someone said to me.

After expressing deep emotional attachment to their homeland, several people in varying degrees of diffidence asked, "Do people know about the Vancouver Asahi in Japan?"

I was taken by surprise. "No, unfortunately, almost no one knows," I confessed.

Those present could not hide their disappointment and disbelief. Moreover, I told them, not many now knew that Japanese had immigrated to Canada.

They were obviously shocked and saddened. I could not meet the eyes of the legendary players present. It was unbearable to face these Asahi heroes, who had yearned for their distant homeland and played to show their pride in being Japanese.

Soon it was time to say goodbye. Made reckless by their sorrow, I immediately vowed to do everything in my power to tell the story of the Vancouver Asahi on my return to Japan.

I had made my big gesture, but time passed without fulfilling my vow. The duty my father had bequeathed me, and the rash promise I made in Canada constantly preyed on my mind. If I don't do something soon, I thought, no one from the Asahi will be left. I've got to carry out my promise while these heroes are still alive.

A reason to start came from a completely unexpected source.

After retiring from the company where I had worked for so many years, I established my own firm. As an independent business consultant, I frequently worked abroad to facilitate deals. In this way I was able to observe Japan, its politics, education and worldview from both macro and micro perspectives. I began to feel an impending sense of crisis for Japan and its future. I came to believe that Japan was about to lose something important.

That was when the Nikkei immigrant experience and the Asahi heroes of the diamond flashed into my mind. The immigrants who crossed the Pacific one hundred years ago were not daunted by rejection or discrimination, however severe. They had found an opening, a way to persevere with pride. The Asahi showed by means of fair play, sportsmanship, and a unique brand of baseball how to transcend racial differences and capture the hearts of everyone who came to know them.

Long ago there was a baseball team of Japanese players in a faraway and unknown land. I wanted to spread their story to as many young people as possible. I firmly believe that the Vancouver Asahi story can inspire people all over the world.

The result is this book, and I have finally been able to keep my promise.

It is an immeasurable loss that Vancouver's Japan Town, its Little Tokyo, has been erased. So much has been tragically lost. When I looked for records and documents about the Asahi, I was surprised that there was so little to be found. In some part, it may be due to my lack of research ability.

The records of the Asahi's one hundred games a year have been lost as well. The scenes I re-created of the Asahi games and other incidents rely on what has been passed down by individual players.

Finally, I would like to apologize to my father, and to everyone connected with the Vancouver Asahi, for the length of time it has taken for me to tell their tale. I give my heart felt thanks to all who encouraged me during the writing of this book.

Ted Y. Furumoto

## Sources

**In Japanese**

**Shinbo, Mitsuru**. *Ishi moto owarruru gotoku nikkei Canada jin shakai shi*, 1975, Tairiku Jihousha.

**Nitta, Jiro**. *Mikkosen suianmaru*, 1982, Kodansha.

**Goto, Norio**. *Nagoya tabunka kenkyukai, dai nanakai kenkyukai nikkei Canada imin to sports*. http://www.geocities.jp/kyouseinagoya/maypage1.html

**In English**

**Adachi, Pat**. *Asahi: A Legend in Baseball*, 2002, Coronet Printing and Publishing, Ltd.

CHAPTER 1

# A Team Is Born

## Powell Street Grounds at Dawn

The city of Vancouver on Canada's western coast is divided north and south by the Burrard Inlet. In the southern part of town there is a sleepy thoroughfare called Powell Street that runs east to west for about three kilometers parallel to the coastline, nestling quietly at the back of lively Chinatown.

Nothing remains of its past. Ninety years ago, though, the area was called either "Japan Town" or "Little Tokyo." Back then it was full of hustle and bustle, and served as the anchor of Vancouver's Japanese community of ten thousand people.

Early one morning in late spring, a boy hurtles out of a house on the east side of Powell Street and runs down the road. He's wearing a baseball uniform and has a school bag slung over one shoulder. He's heading toward the Powell Street Grounds. His teammates had been at practice since dawn's light—five a.m., because the sun rose fast in the early summer.

Far behind the running boy, the mountains across the Burrard Inlet are still capped with snow. Although winter is long gone, lacy white strands float through the air like summer snowflakes. The cottonwood trees have released their seeds, and the downy puffs wafting in the air are harbingers of Vancouver's early summer—and baseball season.

After running full speed down Powell Street, the boy gasps for breath as he hurries onto the field.

"You're late," the coach says gruffly.

"I'm sorry, coach."

"Well, hurry up and get out there!"

The boy quickly digs into his bag, pulls out on his spikes and glove, and puts them on. Jamming his cap on his head, he jumps to join his teammates as shouts and cheers in a mixture of Japanese and English ring out across the field.

"Hey, nice pitch!"

"I dare you to try that again!"

The Powell Street Grounds they're playing on is a ball field in name only—really just a patch of dirt covered with pebbles and weeds. And the nine boys are chasing the ball so hard that they're raising clouds of dust.

The uniforms they wear have an impressive capital "A" embroidered on the left side of the chest. That simple logo stands for the Vancouver Asahi, a team that would be famous in the years to come. The boys hard at play are the Asahi's original nine.

When practice ends, the boys change clothes right there on the field, since there are no showers or locker rooms. Those who have school head for class, and those who work head for their jobs.

As usual, someone says, "Hey, we played pretty well today." And as they leave the Powell Street Grounds, the boys say what they always say: "Let's play again tomorrow!"

## A Man Called Basha Matsu

The Vancouver Asahi team was conceived in Little Tokyo just before World War I. More Japanese had been settling in and around Powell Street, many with second-generation Canadian-born children, so the population of kids in Little Tokyo had swelled. Observing that in white society adults used club sports to educate and guide children, leaders in the Japanese community decided to do the same.

The consensus was that establishing a baseball club was the first priority. The community reached out to a man named Matsujiro Miyazaki to build and coach the team. Nicknamed "Basha Matsu" because of his boundless enthusiasm, extraordinary drive and strength of will, Miyazaki had originally immigrated to Hawaii before coming to Vancouver, where he managed a thriving clothing store and grocery at 200 Powell Street.

Matsujiro readily agreed, and began his search for promising players, asking people if they knew any boys who were both physically gifted and loved baseball.

"There's going to be a baseball club for Japanese kids," he'd tell them, "and the club will provide the uniforms, gear and everything else they need."

Talk of the youth baseball club spread in a hurry throughout the community, and the response far exceeded Matsujiro's expectations.

"Please consider my son for your team," said a man who stopped Matsujiro on Powell Street one afternoon. "He loves baseball, and I can guarantee that he's good. Please!" The man put his rough fisherman's hands together and bowed deeply.

It wasn't just one man, either. Plenty of families wanted their sons on the team, and besieged Matsujiro with fervent pleas.

Although impressed and happy that the team was arousing such enthusiasm, Matsujiro began to have second thoughts. The budget wasn't big enough to pay for a large squad, so he knew there were going to be plenty of disappointed folks.

He also didn't want a team made up of friends who just played for fun. Since he couldn't grant the wishes of all the boys who wanted to be on the squad, he decided the only way to make up for it was to organize an elite team that met everyone's expectations.

"I'll create a baseball team that will overwhelm everyone," Matsujiro said.

The new ball club took shape in 1914, and as Matsujiro had intended it was filled with the finest young baseball talent Vancouver's Japanese community had to offer. The original team had nine boys, the bare minimum they could field. Most were second-generation Japanese born in Canada, but there were also a few boys of around fifteen who had just emigrated from Japan. The players were young, waiting to be molded.

To signify the spirit of the sun rising to light the world, the new team was named the Vancouver Asahi-gun (Vancouver Morning Sun), or Vancouver Asahi for short.

Many of the Asahi's original nine members and their coaches, ca. 1915
Back row, from left: Fukunaga, Matsujiro "Harry" Miyasaki, Takeo Asai, unidentified
Middle row, from left: Ken Suzuki, Tony Kodama, Mickey Kitagawa, Tom Matoba
Front row, from left: Teddy Furumoto, unidentified, Yo Horii, Jim Tabata, Shima

## Diamond Days

The year the Vancouver Asahi team was formed, nineteen-year-old Babe Ruth signed his first professional baseball contract. The Babe made the transition from the minors to the majors that same year, joining the Boston Red Sox and becoming a star before the momentous trade that sent him to the New York Yankees in 1920.

The major leagues were entering a golden age. Even fans in Japan knew the Babe and other top American ballplayers of the day like Ty Cobb, Walter Johnson and George Sisler.

Baseball fever doesn't recognize national borders, so the sport naturally spread to Canada. Baseball was massively popular there, and many teams—from sandlot amateurs to professional outfits to major-league farm teams—proliferated throughout the country.

When people think of Canadian national sports today, ice hockey and Canadian football immediately come to mind. In Toronto and other big east coast cities, interest was rising back then in these new sports. But compared to baseball, ice hockey and football were still minor pastimes.

And baseball was wildly popular in Vancouver, still only a provincial burg on the remote west coast. In fact, baseball monopolized the town. It helped that Vancouver was filled with vacant lots, because as long as there was an empty lot, you could play the game. The field at Powell, while far from ideal, was still considered one of the better venues.

On Saturdays and Sundays, both children and adults in Vancouver watched or played baseball. There were office teams, regional teams, semi-pro and professional teams, and youth clubs. Promoters gathered teams, organized leagues, sold tickets, and put on games.

The objective of many teams was to get good enough to join a league. Players, professional and amateur alike, wanted to play in a popular league where they'd be noticed and perhaps even rise to hero status.

It was a time when all of Vancouver breathed, ate and lived baseball. The Japanese community was no exception. The Vancouver Asahi team sprouted in this hothouse atmosphere.

## A Language in Common

For the record, baseball was introduced to Japan in 1872. It is thought that Howard Wilson, an American teacher employed at Kaisei Junior High School—the predecessor of the University of Tokyo—first put a baseball in the hands of his students.

So baseball got its start as a game for elite students in Japan. However, much like in the United States, it took no time at all for baseball to permeate the country and become a national pastime, form of entertainment, and integral part of the fabric of Japanese life.

Japanese immigration to Canada at the beginning of the twentieth century was concentrated in British Columbia. From the Okanagan Valley in the foothills of the Rocky Mountains to Ocean Falls in the north and Fanny Bay on Vancouver Island, even areas far from Vancouver were attracting Japanese immigrants looking for work.

Wherever the immigrants gathered, regardless of the size of the community, baseball came along. On days off, holidays and work breaks, they would exchange their work tools for bats and gloves and play ball.

In 1908, Japanese immigrants in Little Tokyo formed a team called the Nippons, the forerunner of the Vancouver Asahi. About twenty youths made up the squad. Like the Asahi eventually would, the Nippons used the Powell Street Grounds for practices and games against other Japanese teams.

The residents of Powell Street loved watching the Nippons. Boys hero-worshipped the team, and many of them started playing baseball with the dream of becoming a Nippons player. The boys who later joined the Vancouver Asahi were no exception.

Hearing that the Japanese played baseball too, white baseball fans also showed interest. Japanese and white spectators alike crowded the Powell Street field on the weekends.

The players on the Nippons were all migrant workers, saving up to return to Japan. They had a lot of experience playing ball in Japan before coming to Canada.

That was no surprise. Back in Japan, the National Secondary School Baseball Tournament—the precursor of the Koshien National High School Championship that's now held every summer and ignites baseball fervor all over the country—debuted in 1915. So it was common for Japanese, immigrants or not, to grow up playing baseball in pickup games, at school, or in a club.

This held great significance for Japanese coming to Canada. The majority of first-generation immigrants were not fluent in English. They lived a narrowly circumscribed lifestyle, working hard and following the old customs. Baseball served as a bond of unity, particularly for the first-generation Nikkei born abroad. And once the community was settled and thriving, the first thing Japanese immigrants did was to start a baseball team. Baseball was also the most powerful means for social exchange and communication with local society, and a way to establish as well as express immigrant identity.

The rules of baseball are the same everywhere. Even if you couldn't speak English, you could play as long as you knew the rules. Once the game starts, the color of your skin or where you were born or what language you speak becomes irrelevant. Ability was the difference in deciding superiority or inferiority, victory or defeat.

The fact that baseball took root very early on in Japan, and that players and fans acquired the common language of this game, were providential factors for the Japanese immigrants arriving in Canada.

### All for the Sake of Pride

The circumstances for immigrants in Hawaii and California were much the same. Matsujiro Miyazaki, the Vancouver Asahi's first coach, intuitively understood the role baseball played for immigrants when he lived in Hawaii. In fact, there was even a Japanese team in Hawaii called the Asahi.

But to Matsujiro, the Japanese teams in Canada—including the popular Nippons—simply weren't good enough. They lacked the ability to dominate. Their status was based on sentiment on the Japanese side, and on novelty appeal to white society on the other.

In 1910, the Vancouver Nippons played against a team with the same name from the Japanese community in Victoria, Vancouver Island. Assuming this game remains in the records, it was their first game against a "foreign" team.

On game day, the Powell Street Grounds were overflowing with excited Japanese.

"Hurray for the Nippons!"

"Which Nippons team are you rooting for?"

"Does it matter? Either way, Japan wins!"

Maybe so, but it was Japanese pitted against Japanese, in a game where both teams shared the same name. It was a family fight, brother against brother, a jeering civil war. It was also city against country, Powell Street versus Victoria, and temperatures were rising.

There were a few talented players on each team, but mediocre play followed mediocre play. To many in the crowd, it was a travesty of a game. A lot of the Vancouver Nippons team players were known to bar-hop and eat their way through Little Tokyo after a game. Spectators, to say nothing of the players, may even have been drinking during the game.

The next day, the local community newspaper disparagingly referred to the game as "Drunkards Baseball," and the tone of the article was just as bitingly sarcastic.

Japan had just won the Russo-Japanese War and entered the circle of the world's major powers, as it had long desired. It is easy to imagine the euphoria at home amplifying the feelings of young people making a new life in a foreign country. The power of saké boosted the high spirits and big talk until the night grew old.

But there was also emptiness, a feeling of being lost deep inside. To live alone in a foreign country, suffering from homesickness, spending hours at hard manual labor, smashing up against the soaring walls of white society, and to what end? To suffer so that hardship could be eased at home? Young men were wound tight with resentment, anger and pent-up frustration.

Matsujiro sympathized, but given the time and the circumstances there was nothing to do but to bear the isolation and frustration. And he couldn't help feeling that there were limitations to the kind of baseball they played. Competing within the closed immigrant community was meaningless. To play in a league with strong white teams and to win the championship—that was the challenge.

Baseball was a way to obtain respect. He wanted to face the best white teams and win fair and square. First, though, it was necessary to create a strong team that the white leagues would pay attention to and even admire.

He entrusted that dream to the second-generation kids. These were youths born and raised in Canada speaking English. They might be poor, but they went to the same high schools as the white kids. They did not suffer from the inferiority complex toward white society that had oppressed their fathers.

Instead, they had acquired the strength and determination to push boundaries. They were Nikkei, conscious and proud of their Japanese ancestry, ripe to form a strong team. Matsujiro wanted the Asahi to break free, to cut through the insular shell of the Japanese community to the outside world of the white majority.

Baseball has an underlying power that goes deeper than simple entertainment. Matsujiro felt that in the core of his being. To him the Vancouver Asahi was a team with a mission, destined to uncover that power.

The team's hard practices continued day after day on the Powell Street Grounds under Matsujiro's vigilant watch. The boys joked and laughed, surprised and happy. They could feel themselves getting stronger, getting better.

All nine were filled with a fierce impatience. The day of their debut game was almost upon them.

CHAPTER 2

# The Journey to Canada

## Fathers of the Asahi

The history of the Vancouver Asahi team is rooted in the history
of Japanese society in Canada. Members of the Asahi team were
second-generation Japanese Canadians. Their fathers were the
immigrant youths who had arrived with little but hopes and dreams.

In 1977, the Canadian government celebrated the 100th anniversary of the beginning of the Japanese-Canadian community, and
formally recognized Manzou Nagano, from Kuchinotsu, Nagasaki
Prefecture, as the country's first Japanese immigrant. It is likely that
Japanese sailors who were shipwrecked or on ships making port calls
had come to Canada before Manzou. However, their objective was
not immigration but to return home.

Manzou had gone to work on a British ship as a boiler mainte-
nance man when he was just nineteen years old. In 1877, when he
was twenty-four, the young sailor had jumped ship when his vessel
reached the Fraser River, south of Vancouver, and ended up in a
small village called New Westminster. Manzou was an illegal alien.

He was also the son of a fisherman. It wasn't long before he was making a living fishing the Fraser River, catching salmon using the traditional Japanese method of throwing nets. The success story of Manzou the Salmon King (Ginsake-O) soon spread throughout Japan.

When Manzou arrived, there was no direct shipping between Canada and Japan. Few Japanese followed in his wake. It was only after 1887 when the transcontinental railway run by the Canadian Pacific Railway reached Vancouver that the number of Japanese making passage to Canada gradually increased. Ships began plying a regularly scheduled Pacific Ocean route between Hong Kong and Vancouver.

What really drew the attention of Japanese wanting to emigrate, though, was the possibility of work. In 1886, the year before the Pacific routes opened up, Vancouver had suffered a huge conflagration, and the greater part of the city was destroyed. City planning began in earnest. Hundreds of new sawmills were completed to meet the demand for lumber used in construction and engineering jobs in and around the city.

So Vancouver was in boomtown mode, fast becoming the entryway to Canada for the Pacific Rim. The city was destined to become an international port, and someone had to help build its railway and harbors.

Naturally, the demand for workers in Vancouver increased rapidly, and the air was filled with purpose and brisk activity. That promising news spread very quickly to Japan.

"They say there's so much work to be had in Vancouver that you can take your pick of jobs," people exclaimed. "And you can make as much in one month there as it takes in a year here!"

Although twenty years had passed since the Meiji Restoration, Japan remained poor. The poverty of the country's farming and fishing villages was acute. There was no work to be had, and people were living hand to mouth. The battles between the shogunate and supporters of the emperor had finally ended, spurring a big jump in population growth.

To alleviate the overflow, the Japanese government encouraged emigration. Even without government support, however, the age of isolation was over. A lot of young people were willing to gamble on making a new life in a strange country, especially if the only other choice was to face unremitting poverty at home.

So it was impossible to ignore the lure of Vancouver, where it was said businesses prospered and jobs were to be had. If you could make it to Vancouver, you could make it rich.

The first wave of immigrants hit Hawaii, followed by even bigger waves to the American mainland. Subsequent waves washed up against Canada's western coast, and people from all over Japan began arriving in boomtown Vancouver.

## The Immigrant Wave, Part 1

However fervent their hopes were, Canada was not paradise for the new Japanese Canadians. And British Columbia, where Vancouver is located, was home to the most intense boycott movement against Orientals in all of Canada.

The Issei—first-generation immigrants—could not speak English. These first immigrants were boys, not men, and were anywhere from fourteen to nineteen years old. They had usually only completed primary school. The majority of Japanese immigrants at that time also had very few technical skills.

Those factors naturally affected the social status of the Japanese. They were a source of cheap labor, and their opportunities were limited to physical labor in occupations such as logging, fishing, farming, railway construction, and trade.

An overwhelming majority of them worked in logging and fishery jobs. Railway construction and mining work conditions were more severe, as jobs were unstable and the pay cheaper.

Most of the first generation of immigrants only intended to stay for a short time. They wanted to return home as heroes. In the meantime, they sent money home as soon as they earned it, and saved the little that was left over.

Only a few planned to settle in Canada from the start and to become farmers. Their numbers would only increase when people began starting families and turned away from the instability of seasonal labor in forestry, fishing, construction and mining, and switch to farming.

They faced racial discrimination and anti-Oriental boycotts, and could only engage in business ventures with Japanese customers. The number of would-be entrepreneurs was therefore quite limited. Logging and sawmill jobs were the most plentiful, as there was a high demand for lumber in Vancouver.

The first-generation workers were in great demand. They were assigned to hard physical labor such as lifting, carrying and piling up heavy lumber. The Issei endured silently, working more than ten hours a day without complaint for much less than the white workers received. Understandably, few workers were as welcome as the Japanese to the sawmill operators.

Logging jobs multiplied as the demand for lumber rose. Logging camps proliferated along the Fraser River, on Vancouver Island, and in the gorges to the north near the Rocky Mountains. There were Japanese working everywhere.

The conditions in the logging camps were worse than those in the sawmills. The men were housed in dilapidated huts. The roofs often leaked, and there were gaps in the walls through which the wind blew. And to be hired, the Japanese had to accept wages that were one-third less than what the white workers received.

Even at such low wages, however, the Issei were earning several times what they could make back in Japan. They swallowed their anger at the conditions, working hard to save as much as they could to send home.

There was nothing left to do but fall exhausted on their bunks. Some groaned, some moved restlessly in their sleep. This was their daily routine.

At the end of the brutal days of hard labor, the men would eat a hasty meal and then gather in a vacant lot with bats and balls. Soon the sounds of a handmade, planed wooden bat hitting a ball, dirt scuffed and kicked, and the thwack of a ball settling into a glove would fill the air, punctuated with cries of "Safe!" "Out!"

After the cries of the opposing teams crisscrossed each other, silence would return to the valley until their enthusiastic shouts broke the stillness again.

The sheer joy of playing baseball soothed the men's hearts and bodies. Soon enough, though, they would return to grappling with gigantic trees whose like could not be found in Japan.

### The Immigrant Wave, Part 2

Along with logging, the industry that provided a living for many Japanese in Canada was fishing. For a time, in fact, it was the main pillar of support for the fledgling immigrant community. Almost a decade after Manzou Nagano jumped ship, many groups of Japanese began making the passage to Canada to chase commercial fishing success.

One man, a carpenter named Gihei Kono, was responsible for this wave of fishermen.

Kono, who was from Mio-mura (Village) in Wakayama Prefecture, set sail for Canada from Yokohama in August 1888. Mio-mura was an ordinary fishing village similar to many on the coast of the Kii Peninsula.

Gihei was different from his fellow villagers, though. He hated the economic uncertainty of fishing, which depended on too many uncontrollable variables. He turned his back on fishing, left the village, and apprenticed in Kyoto to become a carpenter.

He also had a pioneering spirit, and dreamt from a young age of starting his own business in a foreign country. Gihei was often asked by his cousin, who was a crewmember on a foreign ship, "Why don't you emigrate to Canada?"

Gihei finally took that advice to heart. Hoping for companions to join him, he approached relatives and friends, but nobody else had any enthusiasm for the venture. Gihei mulled it over, and finally decided to set out for Canada on his own.

He landed in Vancouver on September 5, twenty days after leaving Yokohama. He promptly set off for Powell Street, where he'd heard that many Japanese lived. What he found was not much of a community—just five or six cheap, dormitory-style hotels where Vancouver's Japanese sawmill workers lived.

While preparing for his journey back in Yokohama, Gihei kept hearing stories from ships' crews about Steveston, a town located on the north side of the mouth of the Fraser River, about twenty kilometers from Vancouver. In his mind, Steveston became a paradise. All Gihei could think about during the voyage to Canada was to get to Steveston. After he picked a hotel to stay at, he promptly asked the owner, "Excuse me, how do you get to Steveston?"

"If you're thinking of working around Vancouver, I hear it's easy to make a living fishing or farming in Steveston," the innkeeper said, and then told him how to get there.

The next day, Gihei swung aboard a wagon headed for Steveston. When he got there, the young adventurer could not believe his eyes. Standing on the shore of the Fraser River, what he thought was a river was so wide he could not see the opposite shore. If he was told it was the ocean he wouldn't have doubted it.

What made it even more unbelievable was that the vast river was completely filled by an enormous school of salmon, fish on top of fish, making its way upriver toward their breeding grounds. Gihei was lost for words looking at the overwhelming sight that seemed not of this world.

At that time only fifteen Japanese settlers lived in Steveston. They fished for salmon in the summer and farmed during the winter. There was good farmland in Sun Valley, about ten kilometers upstream.

But what caught Gihei's imagination was the salmon fishing, not farming. After just a quick look around, he realized the number of boats going out was unusually small. Yet the salmon seemed numberless—and it appeared there was unlimited room for newcomers.

What crossed his thoughts were the fishermen back in his hometown of Mio-mura. No matter how hard you worked in Japan, it was impossible to escape from poverty. Here the work would be equally hard, but it would be possible to make real money and better your lot. The lives of the villagers would improve tremendously. Thinking of this, Gihei could not keep still.

A casual comment from one of the Japanese immigrants in Steveston just poured more oil on the fire.

"The white men only fish for sockeye," the man told him with a shrug.

The sockeye salmon caught in the Fraser River was canned, his companion explained, and exported to Britain and Australia. Other types of salmon were apparently of no interest. Only sockeye was considered profitable, and only part of the fish was canned. Everything else, from head to guts to roe, was tossed into the river.

Gihei remembered seeing the fishery companies, called canneries, which dotted the shores of the Fraser River. So those canneries throw away roe like garbage, he thought. Not only that, they ignore the Chinook king salmon, the Coho, chum, and dog salmon! The absolute waste astounded him.

Though he'd often been called a braggart at home due to his high-flying talk, Gihei's entrepreneurial spirit was aroused. Salmon other than the sockeye could be had for the taking.

Gihei felt that he had just stumbled upon an unexpected gold-mine. Scooping up the salmon, salting them, and exporting them to Japan could make him a fortune.

Everything fell into place for Gihei as he remembered the stories about Manzou Nagano, who had immigrated to Canada ten years before him. Manzou had become extremely wealthy, and had been called the Salmon King, or more specifically, the King of Salted Salmon.

Gihei hurried back to Powell Street and sent word at once to his fellow villagers about what he'd seen at the Fraser River.

The attitude of the villagers who had previously refused to emigrate changed completely upon hearing Gihei's news. The following year, Gihei's younger brother and many villagers, including relatives, left for Steveston. They were the vanguard of Mio-mura villagers who would depart every year around salmon-fishing season.

Rumors of the incredible salmon fishing on the Fraser River leapt from Mio-mura to other fishing villages.

"In Canada, the salmon fill the rivers."

"Hoist a flag in the middle of the salmon and it'll go upstream without falling over."

"The river's so full of salmon a dog can ride upstream on their backs."

The rumors swelled expectations and spread. Following the example of Mio-mura's folk, fishermen set out for Canada from villages all along Japan's Pacific coast, from Tohoku in the north to southern Kyushu and the many islands of the Seto Inland Sea. It was the Great Salmon Rush, a dream of thousands of pieces of gold.

Of course the immigrants to the new land of opportunity were not limited to fishermen in those locations. There were several groups from Setouchi as well. The parents of the Vancouver Asahi's first ace pitcher, Teddy Furumoto, came all the way from Oshima County, Yamaguchi Prefecture, on the tip of Honshu.

Teddy Furumoto
One of the original nine of the Asahi, Teddy was equally adept as a
pitcher, shortstop and right fielder.

At a much later time, having heard that he was recruiting players for the Asahi baseball team, a man approached Matsujiro, the team's first manager-coach, saying "Please put my son on the team." He was one of the young fishermen who came from one of the islands in Setouchi to Vancouver.

Ornate homes arose in Mio-mura and other fishing villages that had sent people to Canada, built with the money the immigrants sent home. Mio-mura and other such villages came to be called "America-mura" or "American villages."

Steveston became a second home for fishermen from Mio-mura and other parts of Japan—a magnetic base camp for Japanese immigrants.

In 1894, six years after Gihei arrived in Canada, the number of Japanese immigrants, including those who came up from the United States for the fishing season, had risen to four thousand.

The Japanese immigrants had also expanded their base of operations from Steveston to Vancouver Island, and to the rivers and coastal regions of Prince Rupert to the north. Besides those fishing for salmon, there were many who went after herring and whale.

These skilled men, born, brought up, and trained in traditional fishing villages, had been fishing since early boyhood. Gradually, it became apparent that white and native fishermen could not compete. An estimated 70 percent of the ships fishing the Fraser River were Japanese. It is no exaggeration to say that the Japanese developed the salmon-fishing industry on the Fraser River.

The white managers of the fishery companies, no fools they, would assert, "No matter who brings in a big catch, they can't beat the Japs."

In every occupation, the position of the Japanese immigrants who were employed for simple physical labor was low. That was also the case for fishermen. There was no change in the hard conditions for physical labor and comparatively low pay.

Still, by dint of their ability and skills, Japanese fishermen were able to surpass white and native fishermen. The Japanese immigrants were able to expand their occupation to a near monopoly. Thus, they were able to group together and insist on fairer compensation from the cannery companies in a systematic way.

It was not only in the fishing industry that the Japanese workers became indispensable. Men who had succeeded economically as well as socially in improving their status became leaders in the immigrant community, further strengthening their influence.

In Canada at that time, however, the Japanese immigrants' success was destined to become the seed of friction before long with the white majority. This was especially so in British Columbia, a state where discrimination and racism were rampant.

## The Beginning of Japan Town

The number of Japanese in Vancouver swelled. Mostly they were workers in sawmills. Optimistic information was passed on from those that had made the passage back to their hometowns. More immigrants followed.

Immigrants from various countries more or less made a similar exodus in this way. However, a key characteristic of Japanese immigrants was their tendency to summon families and neighbors collectively.

The ships carrying immigrants sailing from Yokohama made their first port call in Victoria, on Vancouver Island. Japanese were already working there as miners, fishermen and loggers. The ship would unload passengers there, and then arrive in Vancouver the next day.

Burrard Inlet was a long and narrow entrance into the port of Vancouver. Mountains over a thousand meters high could be seen on the left-hand side when approaching the city. On the right, Gastown extended into the mist. Gastown was named after Gassy Jack Deighton, who arrived with a barrel of whiskey and promptly set up a saloon in the area before the city was named Vancouver.

After disembarking, immigrants walked from the tip of the pier to a big plaza with a railroad track. There stood a building that combined an immigration center with a freight warehouse. Once the immigrants completed their entry formalities here, they headed on foot to Powell Street, which was just a hop, skip and jump away.

A Japanese consulate opened in Vancouver in 1889, two years after a regularly scheduled sea route between Yokohama and

Vancouver was established. The establishment of the consulate was proof of the increasing number of immigrants to Canada. That same year, a boy was born to Washiji and Yao Ooya. This child, named Kanji, was the first of the Canadian-born second generation.

At that time, there were three sawmills operating in Vancouver. The largest, near Powell Street, was Hastings Sawmill. It is said that over a hundred Nikkei worked there at a time.

It was impossible to accommodate the flow of immigrants with the pre-existing five or six dormitory-style hotels. In 1891, Shozo Ishikawa, originally from Yokohama, opened three new inns designated as "Japan Rooms."

In many of these dormitory-style hotels, punnets—low, flat baskets that barely accommodated one adult—were laid out in the rooms. There are tales of sleeping in this way that have been passed down by lodgers. These establishments could not be properly called inns, and barely fit the definition of lodging houses. They were said to be suitable only as protection from inclement weather.

In any case, the number of Japanese immigrants multiplied in the Powell Street area, including those rooming-house tenants. Businesses that provided services and goods indispensable to daily living became necessary. Little by little, immigrants starting opening small shops along Powell Street. This was the beginning of Japan Town.

The foundation for Japan Town, or Little Tokyo, had been roughly completed by about 1910. Little Tokyo ran north and south for about four hundred meters between East Hastings and Railway Streets, and about five hundred meters east and west between Main and Princess streets.

The central thoroughfare of the area, Powell Street, was lined for hundreds of meters on both sides with three-story buildings in the Western architectural style of brick masonry. It was surely a spectacular sight for those who made the passage from the Japanese countryside. The first floor was generally used as a store while the second and third stories became hotels or rooming houses, the majority run by Japanese.

Everything a Japanese person needed for daily life could be found along Powell Street. The avenue was lined with gift shops and stores offering staples such as rice, fresh noodles, tofu, and boiled fish paste. There were also restaurants, cafés, public baths, tailor shops, haberdasheries, laundries, medical clinics, barbershops, drugstores, sheet metal factories, and churches.

The road was a magnet that attracted Japanese living outside Vancouver as well. Young Japanese men who worked in the sawmills and fishing and lumber camps of the northern interior regularly descended on Little Tokyo for much-needed rest and recreation.

Japanese fresh off the boat mingled with the Nikkeijin on the store-lined main thoroughfare. Wagons loaded with luggage constantly came and went. If you stepped into the back streets, though, you would find a quieter residential area for the Nikkei. Surrounded by their countrymen, it was a home away from home.

While there were other small communities of Japanese Canadians in Vancouver, the only area with the scale and size to be called Little Tokyo was around Powell Street. It remains Canada's first, and only, Japan Town.

A generational change in the community was coming, a shift from the first arrivals to a generation who regarded Canada as their home. After the prohibition against single male immigrants was put into effect in 1907, the number of families settling in Little Tokyo grew, and the area became overcrowded.

**CHAPTER 3**

# A Storm of Adversity

## The Gathering Tempest

The Japanese would emigrate in groups, either related families or neighbors, from the same town or village, and settle together, keeping the same interpersonal relationships as in their hometowns.

Earlier arrivals looked after later immigrants, advising and helping with jobs and homes. They represented an indispensable lifeline for those that crossed the sea without a word of English, depending on family or friends who had gone on before them.

Immigrants to Canada came from all over Japan, although the majority came from Yamagata, Hiroshima, Fukuoka, Kumamoto and Yamagata prefectures. In Vancouver, however, over half of the immigrants were from Shiga Prefecture.

Shiga was known throughout Japan as the center of the famous Omi merchant peddlers. While immigrants from the other prefectures typically worked as fishermen or as loggers and sawmill laborers, those from Shiga Prefecture were entrepreneurs in commerce and business. This tradition continued in Vancouver.

In a Powell Street bar:

"Hey, young man. You must be new in town. Where are you from?" asked a man who seemed to know his way around of a young man who looked fresh off the boat.

"I'm from Higo, sir."

"Well, Higo-san, I'm from near Mie. Best regards to you."

It wasn't unusual at the time for people to call each other by the names of their hometowns or prefectures. It seemed silly to be so concerned about someone's origins when everyone was sharing the experience of making a new life in a new land, but where people came from back home had vast importance. There were words that indicated a shared prefecture (*ku-mono*), and a shared hometown (*mura-mono*), conveying a closeness and intimacy usually associated with family.

On the other hand, people from different prefectures were called *yoso-mono* or outsiders. Relations with outsiders were strained. This was the dark aspect of an insular and closed Japanese society.

In 1902, immigrants from Hiroshima formed the first prefectural association. Other prefectural associations followed soon after. Within a decade there were more than twenty such associations.

In the Japanese community, the greater the number of association members, the greater the association's influence. In Vancouver, the immigrants from Shiga Prefecture were a swaggering presence in the Powell Street area.

Disputes arising from differences in origin revealed an increasing exclusivity. It didn't seem to matter whether there was a real reason to fight. Hostility was expressed over differences in prefectures or even towns within a prefecture.

In the Issei community, physical fights were commonplace. Who fought who changed constantly. People not only fought over their origins, they warred about such factors as the different sects and temples of Buddhism.

Alcohol, gambling, women . . . temptation was rife for single young men far away from home and earning wages several times higher than in Japan. There were those willing to cheat or otherwise take advantage of their countrymen.

Once a Nikkeijin quit a job, the company would never hire them again. Some immigrants would blow their pay in Little Tokyo, then go and find another job. More than a few ended up with no place to go. The cheap rooming houses and hotels of Little Tokyo were where the migrant workers congregated, the jobless at loose ends like duckweed in a pond.

To take a step outside the familiar confines of the Japanese community was to come face to face with rampant discrimination and prejudice. The anger of the young men was turned back on their own community. Looking for an outlet for their pent-up frustration meant an escalation of fighting for fighting's sake.

Many Nikkei in Little Tokyo, sympathetic to their plight, tried to help the jobless drifters return to a normal life. Employers found the Japanese workers useful, since the immigrants worked diligently for cheap wages. However, as the number of immigrants grew, the attitudes of Canadian society began to change.

This was very similar to what occurred with immigrants from China, who were the first Asian settlers in Canada. They had come either directly from China or via the United States. The majority worked for very low wages, helping to construct the transcontinental railroads. No matter how indispensable and convenient cheap labor was to big companies, however, white Canadians soon began to fear the loss of their own jobs. Before long, Canada would shut out the Chinese.

Japanese workers filled the gap the Chinese left, expanding employment opportunities beyond the fishing, logging and commerce open to them. But it was just a matter of time before those opportunities closed.

To Anglo-Canadian society, however, the Chinese and Japanese were interchangeable. Both were outsiders. The gut feeling white Canadians held regarding the immigrants was that the outsiders should return to their own countries once their work was done. This feeling was especially strong in British Columbia, which was closest to Asia across the Pacific Ocean and where many Asian immigrants had settled.

In addition, Canada's west coast held a special meaning for the white majority. Europeans had settled eastern Canada, which was closer to Europe, from the 16th and 17th centuries. In comparison, the west coast was not developed until the 19th century. There was no direct route connecting Canada's east and west coasts until the latter half of the 19th century.

The Panama Canal, which would not open to traffic until 1914, had not yet been completed, so there were only two routes from the east coast of Canada to the west coast. The land route meant crossing the United States from east to west, then traveling north. The sea route required a voyage around South America's Cape Horn, then northward on the Pacific Ocean. In either case, the journeys were hard and roundabout.

Much like their ancestors who had bade farewell to Europe and obtained land in North America, the white settlers on the west coast left the long-developed east coast for a pristine frontier. A considerable number of settlers came imagining a new paradise.

In comparison to the hardships white settlers suffered on the arduous overland and sea routes, Asian immigrants had a much more direct voyage across the Pacific. To the white settlers, it seemed as if the Asian immigrants landed in crashing waves to expand throughout the west coast.

The way things were going, it seemed that British Columbia, supposed to be a white paradise, would not remain so for much longer. Various fears and worries, founded and unfounded, beset white society in British Columbia.

The government of British Columbia passed a bill in 1895 that denied citizens of Asian descent the right to vote. Shortly prior to this bill, Japanese immigrants were also required to become naturalized Canadian citizens to obtain work.

## Eating Cat Food

Naturalization was required, but it came with certain restrictions. The natural rights of citizenship were denied even if naturalized. The message was clear: We don't want you here.

The majority of the first-generation Issei actually had no intention of staying. They were in Canada to work and send money home, and at the end of their lives they intended to return to Japan and live in comfort. They were also not comfortable with the idea of naturalization. However, this affected their ability to earn a wage, so they steeled themselves and became citizens. Yet they were denied the same rights that other Canadian citizens possessed. This was discrimination plain and simple, and the Japanese immigrants were disappointed, frustrated and angry.

On the other hand, from the white point of view, the Japanese were not only cheap laborers who took jobs that might have gone to white workers, they were also hard to get to know, individually and collectively. They were insular and congregated in one place. It did not seem as if they were of a mind to learn English, or even interact with Canadian society.

When many Japanese children reached school age, they would return to Japan with their mothers to receive national compulsory education. After graduating, they would come back to Canada as migrant workers. Those children who did not return to Japan went to Japanese school in Japan Town and were taught in the Japanese language. How could the Japanese become true Canadian citizens in this way? White society felt it was impossible to build friendly relationships with them.

The problem became more complex when differences in culture and lifestyle came into play. For example, the Issei, who had brought their miso, rice, kettles, and rice cooking pots with them, made no attempt to adapt their eating habits in any way. Their meals included rice, pickles, cooked fish, and miso soup, without fail.

This was very natural for the Japanese, but it was very different from prevailing white culture and customs. Just this difference in food and eating habits was enough for white Canadians to distrust the Japanese. Japanese food was considered disgusting and not fit to eat.

One evening, several white men forced their way into a home in Little Tokyo. It was so sudden that there was little resistance. The men were obviously there to bully and frighten. They pointed at the dinner laid out on the table. "Hey look! This isn't food for humans." "This is cat food! You must be animals!"

On the table sat grilled, salted dog salmon and bowls of salmon roe over rice. It is true that no one but the Japanese ate such food in Canada. These ingredients were usually either thrown away or sold to cat and dog food manufacturers. "We could endure any hardship, but it was impossible to endure the racism," remembered a Japanese immigrant long after that time.

The division between the white and Japanese communities grew wider. And once the fuses of racism and prejudice were lit, the fires would not die out.


## Strikebreakers

Anti-Japanese discrimination directly affected workplaces in the fishing and logging industries.

There were three types of Japanese immigrants who fished for a living. The first type obtained a fishing license, and then arranged everything necessary from gear to a boat to fish commercially at their own expense. The second fished with a boat and gear the canneries provided in exchange for food and a house. The third got a salary from the canneries for catching and processing fish.

The first type of fisherman naturally made the most profit, but fishing licenses were not issued without proof of naturalization. They also needed a moderate amount of money to arrange for all the necessary equipment and a boat.

Although many Japanese fishermen owned or leased boats and fished independently, the majority worked for companies that provided boats and gear. Very few Japanese worked for just a salary.

For any fisherman, however, the return was never as much as expected because the Canadian government limited the number of fish caught annually as a means of resource conservation.

Time was also a factor. The fishing season lasted five months from July to January 1. During this period, only fifty-five days of fishing were allowed.

Engine-powered fishing boats were also prohibited. This meant that most fishing was done in small boats with two-man crews. Both rowed to a fishing point, where one would control the boat while the other fished using nets.

The prices the fishery companies paid for a Japanese fishermen's catch was lower than what white fishermen got. Thus, even if a fisherman was independent, the money left after deducting operating costs was low. The money made by fishermen who used company boats and equipment was even lower, as those costs were deducted.

In short, no Japanese could make a living just by fishing. The men also worked in sawmills, in railroad construction and other jobs during the winter after the fishing season ended. If they did not do so, they would barely be able to send any money back to their families in Japan.

Some fishermen lived on a rough type of houseboat on the Fraser River. These were rafts that had huts or shacks constructed on them. They were cheap to maintain and popular. The rafts were also home, and the fishermen would move the raft from sawmills to logging camps along the river during the winter months, and move near the mouth of the river near the canneries when the fishing season started.

The problem was that the Japanese fishermen accepted such poor working conditions.

As stated previously, the Japanese fishermen were skilled, and would accept low wages as long as they were able to work. white fishermen did not go to sea when the sea was rough. Fish prices would rise at such times. Japanese fishermen would deliberately set out to catch fish during bad weather.

For fishery companies, no fishermen were as convenient as the Japanese. It was natural that Japanese would come to make up the majority of fishermen on the Fraser River.

To white and native fishermen, the Japanese fishermen were fools for work. The latter would work all hours from morning to night, going out in all kinds of weather. There was no way to compete.

The goal of the Japanese fishermen, just as for any Issei, was to secure work, and send as much money as possible home before finally returning to Japan. This was very different from the white and native people's objective, which was to secure a steady job under the best possible conditions.

In the spring of 1900, white and native fishermen decided to strike against the canneries for higher prices for their hauls. They approached the Japanese to take part in a united strike. "All fishermens' lives are on the line. Strike with us!"

They also asked the Japanese fishing cooperative to participate. The cooperative was initially sympathetic, but the cannery companies made their countermove. The Japanese immigrants were in a weak position.

When the strike began, the canneries cut off food supplies and threatened eviction from company housing. The Japanese could not afford to strike, so they went back to work.

To the strikers, this was blatant strikebreaking by Japanese scabs. To the Japanese, it was a means for survival. The strikers had reached out to the Japanese fishermen, despite fears that the Japanese would take jobs away from them. The Japanese rejection of a united strike resulted in accumulated anger, to later explode in fury.

That the Japanese were in British Columbia at all was perceived as the root of all evil. The white fishermen appealed to the provincial government and pushed hard to shut out the Japanese. Antipathy towards Asian immigration fueled the appeal. Even the canneries that had welcomed Japanese immigrants as cheap labor and a means to divide and conquer strikes could not stand in the way of the gathering momentum.

Fishing licenses were denied, and cannery companies would not employ Japanese immigrants. Fishermen of Japanese descent would gradually disappear from Canada's west coast.

Much the same happened in logging and other jobs. The Japanese immigrants, who expanded employment opportunities by accepting low wages, were cut off from jobs. This immigrant strategy for employment was no longer possible.

### Riot and Aftermath

In 1900, thirty years after Manzou Nagano came ashore as the first Japanese immigrant to arrive in Canada, an event that changed the immigrants' lives occurred in Vancouver. An anti-Japanese movement in the neighboring United States directly triggered the event—

a bill presented to the San Francisco city assembly that called for banishing Japanese and other Asians.

Fortunately, the legislation did not pass. But in 1905 the Asiatic Exclusion League was formed in California. The exclusion movement spread from California to other states and spurred a similar movement in Canada.

In February 1907, The United States prohibited immigrants from coming to the American mainland via Hawaii, Mexico and Canada. It was a policy specifically aimed at Japanese immigrants.

Immigrants from Japan to the United States typically landed first in Hawaii. If there was no work to be found in Hawaii, the next step was to travel to the American mainland, where wages were higher. Beginning in 1890, this trajectory was to become ever more common.

When Japanese immigrants were suddenly prohibited from making the passage to the American mainland, some chose to go to Canada. Matsujiro Miyasaki, the first manager of the Vancouver Asahi, may have been among those who chose this route.

Every month a ship from Hawaii would carry close to three hundred Japanese immigrants to the port of Vancouver. This fanned the fears of white supremacists. "The way things are going, this country will be really taken over by Japs!"

"What can we do about it?"

The situation was volatile. The leaders of the exclusion movement were searching for a good reason to spur the expansion of their cause. They found one on July 24, 1907.

As usual, a ship from Hawaii arrived in Vancouver carrying Japanese immigrants. However, the number of immigrants it carried was several times the usual number. Close to twelve hundred Japanese, the largest group so far, were about to land in Vancouver.

This galvanized the exclusion movement. One of its representatives was Robert Bowser, the attorney general of British Columbia. Although he knew otherwise, he made inflammatory remarks in the state legislature.

"Don't be surprised by 1200 immigrants, because research predicts that 50,000 immigrants will be coming within this year!"

To ensure that his assertions would be believed, he lied and distorted facts. "The Japanese commissioner of immigration will come to Vancouver soon. I have heard that his purpose is to make preparations for the reception of large numbers of immigrants."

The Japanese commissioner of immigration the attorney general referred to was actually Kikujiro Ishii, head of the International Trade Bureau of the Ministry of Foreign Affairs. His purpose in visiting Vancouver was to investigate and understand the realities of immigrant life.

At that time, around seventy thousand Anglo Canadians were living in Vancouver. Thinking that the attorney general would not be making baseless statements, a large majority of the population fell into a panic.

The immigration issue increasingly rocked Vancouver, and A.E. Fowler of the Japanese and Korean Exclusion League, a central figure in the American expulsion movement, tried to take advantage of the growing fears. An organization to exclude Asian immigrants was formed in Vancouver. Politicians, including city assemblymen as well as the provincial governor, doctors, lawyers, businessmen, church leaders and labor union leaders all joined in the movement. Several thousand people, from the top levels of British Columbia's government to average citizens added their names to the movement's membership list.

This happened during the first ten days of August. And then something much worse happened on September 7, 1907. The Vancouver Asiatic Exclusion League planned their first rally during Kikujiro Ishii's visit to Vancouver.

People began to gather throughout the afternoon in a city park that was the starting point of the rally. By the early evening, the crowd exceeded five thousand people. City officials and clergymen rode in a wagon at the head of the march. The crowd, supplied with placards reading "For a white Canada" followed. The marchers headed for city hall.

About four thousand workers formed the majority of the crowd, called to participate by the labor unions. It was an impressive show intended to illustrate how many were affected by Japanese immigration, and the extent of the unity of support for Asian exclusion.

Before long, the parade of demonstrators arrived at city hall. Anti-Japanese speeches were to be delivered at 7 p.m., and the event was scheduled to end with a resolution to ban Asian immigration.

City hall could only hold about half the crowd, however, so thousands milled about outside, waiting about an hour for the speeches inside to end. One man leapt on to the steps of city hall in front of the crowd to make a speech, calling for a stop to Asian immigration and the expulsion of all Asians from both America and Canada. The man was A. E. Fowler from Seattle.

"Drive out the Orientals!" he cried. "For a white Canada!"

His words struck chords of anger in the crowd. What are we doing here? We're here to be doing something about it! The crowd responded to the inflammatory demagogue, and began turning into a mob. "That's right! Drive them out!" "For a white Canada!"

The crowd outside began chanting in chorus and marching in file. Before anyone realized it, the agitator from Seattle was in control of the local extremists.

The atmosphere was that of a heated witchhunt. It was now a completely different crowd from the one that had arrived at city hall.

Inside, speeches by local leaders and dignitaries continued. No one inside had the slightest inkling of what was happening outside with the crowd.

The mob left city hall and headed north toward East Pender Street, where Chinatown was located. Japan Town was a little past Chinatown.

As the head of the mob reached Chinatown, someone in the mob threw a stone. A sharp crack sounded very loudly in the dim light as the stone broke the glass storefront of a Chinese restaurant. By chance, this became the signal that triggered the riot. Rocks and stones were hurled. The sounds of breaking glass and the roaring mob filled the night. They were out of control. The Chinese locked their doors and barricaded themselves inside their homes. There was no resistance, and the Chinese could only wait quietly until the violence stopped.

The mob raged back and forth through Chinatown. Once they were satisfied that nothing further could be destroyed, there was a brief moment of satisfaction. Then the agitators whipped the mob into a frenzy again with shouts of "Let's get the Japs! The Japs are the enemy!" "Let's kill the Japs!"

It was now 8:30 at night. The mob resembled a giant crawling caterpillar as it made its way a few hundred meters north of Chinatown, where Little Tokyo began at Powell Street.

When the horde came to the western edge of Little Tokyo, they began to throw stones and rocks at the first store on the corner. This was before Little Tokyo was paved, so there was plenty of ammunition lying about on the ground. The mob quickly wrecked the corner store. Feeling indestructible, the shouting crowd headed toward the eastern edge of Little Tokyo, rampaging through the streets.

The Japanese were stunned by the sudden, unexpected invasion as the mob shuttled back and forth between Little Tokyo and Chinatown.

The leaders of Little Tokyo gathered together as soon as the mob turned back. Measures were debated on what to do for the next attack. "The mob might return. Someone go scout and see what's happening."

Two or three young men slipped out to follow the mob. After a while they returned, reporting that "they're not breaking up and they'll definitely be coming back."

Meanwhile, the white mob was looting Chinatown. Many in the mob broke into stores for alcohol and food. Once reason has disintegrated and violence is sanctioned, it is not so easy to return to rational behavior.

The mob was restless, insatiable, hungry for violence. The Japanese had been too taken by surprise to resist. Their lack of resistance was disappointing to the mob, which longed to show the Japanese who was really in power. There was nothing to show the Japanese commissioner of immigration.

The mob was of one mind. "This time we go to battle. We'll show those Japs!" This was the moment when the mob found its focus again, agitators or no agitators. With new energy, the mob headed for Little Tokyo.

In Little Tokyo, the people were hastily preparing to repel the unruly invaders at all costs.

Scouts were dispatched to report on the mob's movements. Lookouts were watching from the roofs of corner buildings. "They'll be back. Women and children, stay inside and stay quiet. No matter what, don't go outside. Men, gather together with weapons."

Men were assigned to run from house to house with the message. Soon, men with whatever could be used as weapons gathered in a shop, which had been designated a temporary headquarters. "This time we won't just take it. Let's show them what true Japanese spirit is."

The men tied on headbands and then ran to their posts after receiving instructions. They gripped clubs, walking sticks, wooden swords, whatever could be used to defend themselves. Among them were some who had casually thrust a Japanese sword in their belts or in a rough rope tied around their waists.

Young fishermen who by chance were staying in cheap lodgings during their off season joined the men. They were young, aggressive, and physically hardened by their work on the boats. Along with the men armed with swords, they would be in the front line of defense.

Barricades blockaded pivotal points and streets. Men raised loads of rocks, stones, and bricks in buckets up to the roofs of corner buildings. Many men climbed to the roof of the store that was the first target of attack. It was thought that the mob would invade Little Tokyo and begin their second attack from this corner.

Not all the women hid themselves inside, either. Some were in charge of food distribution, while others packed and distributed glass bottles filled with sand.

As the defense took shape by one strategy and another, the white mob arrived on the western edge of Powell Street. In front of the mob were barricades. On the rooftops were men brandishing bricks and stones. It was a completely different scene from their first foray. In the short time available, the formerly defenceless Little Tokyo had been turned into a fortress, crude though it may have been. Some in the mob hesitated momentarily. However, on the whole, the rabble's response was enthusiastic. If the Japs want to fight, so much the better! We'll put an end to this. As they rushed the corner, though, stones and bricks were flung on their heads.

The rush stopped momentarily, the mob crouching from the onslaught. Men bayed in anger, and the mob forced their way through the barricade. The front line of the Japanese defense lay in wait, armed with swords, clubs, and wooden swords.

The unsheathed Japanese swords gleamed in the darkness. The defenders stood waiting, ferocious and determined. It is said that the first man to run was a policeman, part of a contingent sent to control the riot.

The men at the head of the mob were also frightened and tried to flee, but no one knew what was happening in the middle and the back of the mob, which was surging forward. The two sides met with a clash. The mob flailed at the Japanese with branches and iron bars. Then a pistol shot rang out. "It's him! He's got a gun!" snarled a Japanese defender. In a moment, the man with the pistol was swarmed by a group of Japanese.

Injuries were being suffered on both sides. When a Japanese man was hurt, someone would pull him back to safety. The fighting went on, however, as someone would take his place and his sword, shouting "Banzai!" The stones and bricks kept flying over, hitting the back of the mob. The situation was clear.

It was difficult for the white agitators to organize a wave of assaults upon the barricades, much less get past them, due to the desperate resolution and fight the Japanese were displaying. The rioters were gradually pushed back toward the vicinity of the entrance to Little Tokyo. The mob's momentum began to waver, and finally broke. They retreated, heading for Chinatown.

The injured among the mob lay on the streets, groaning. The mounted police were finally able control the rioters and help the injured.

The repulsed and disgraced white mob could not calm down. The remaining part of the mob tried to invade Little Tokyo again, but the Japanese defenders in their headbands remained alert and on guard all night, barring the entrances to Little Tokyo. Even then the riot did not end so easily. The mounted police began to push the rioters back. The rioters finally lost their will to fight, and finally scattered.

Fortunately, according to the newspapers, there were no deaths and the number of injured was lower than it could have been.

Ironically, it was Chinatown, where there was no resistance, that the damage was most devastating. The Canadian government quickly responded to claims for compensation of damages suffered at the hands of the rioters. As a result, the Japanese received amounts close to, if not over, the amount of restitution requested. It appears that the Chinese were not able to obtain full compensation so easily, however, as not all of their claims were reimbursed.

At that time, Japan was an imperial ally of Great Britain, and thus, by extension, an ally of Canada, which was part of the British Empire. There was therefore a difference in how the Canadian government responded to the claims of the two Asian immigrant groups.

## Hard Times

The true impact of the Vancouver race riot fell upon the Japanese immigrants. They had united in confronting and defending themselves against a white mob. The mob was clearly in the wrong, and even some white people thought as much. However, they were only a handful, not the majority. The misinterpreted image of a Japanese as "barbarous and militant" spread throughout white society. "How much longer before such dangerous immigrants will be thrown out of Canada?"

The majority of white Canadians were not aware of the realities of life for Japanese immigrants. As a result, their fear and mistrust of the Japanese kept increasing. Tension was in the air.

Under strong pressure from the Canadian government, Japan entered discussions in January 1908 to limit the number of immigrants. The Hayashi-Lemieux Agreement, partially named after the Canadian labor minister of who negotiated it, cut the number of Japanese who could make the passage to Canada to work to four hundred people annually.

Until that time, over a thousand Japanese had come and gone freely between Japan and Canada every year. The Canadian government thought this would eventually decrease the number of Japanese immigrants remaining in Canada. This was true to a certain extent, but the government miscalculated. The new regulations had a crucial loophole: the restriction did not include the immediate family of an immigrant already in Canada. Instead of leaving Canada after a lifetime of work to return to a well-deserved retirement back in Japan, the immigrants made the choice to bring their parents, wives and children to Canada to settle.

The decision to settle in Canada was not made just by men who were already married. To take advantage of the loophole, single men would arrange to be married. A single immigrant man would exchange photographs with a single woman living in Japan. If both sides agreed, a marriage was arranged, and the bride would set sail at once. This was the "picture bride" system. The number of Japanese newlyweds increased in Canada.

The picture bride system caused various tragicomedies because of gaps between the images in the photographs and reality. Nonetheless, this bride search method became widespread among the single immigrants. The Hayashi-Lemieux Agreement, which meant to drive out the Japanese, had the opposite effect of persuading Japanese to settle in Canada.

The Canadian government did not loosen restrictions on immigration, however, and in fact lowered the number of admissible immigrants every year. In 1928, the admissible number of immigrants, including parents and wives, was 150 people. At this rate, it was possible that Canada would refuse Japanese immigrants completely within a decade.

The character of Japanese society in Canada gradually began to change as well. Fewer immigrants planned to leave Canada for Japan after retirement, and the number of immigrants who intended to settle and become Canadians grew rapidly. The second-generation kids were growing up in Little Tokyo, among them some who would become trailblazers in various fields, but those individuals were still very much the exception.

Anti-Japanese prejudice was still the norm in Anglo-Canadian society, and the opening of the door to Japanese assimilation within Canadian society was yet to come. The Nikkei suffered from intense racism and discrimination until well after World War II.

It was only natural that a strong desire for a symbol of Nikkei pride welled up within Canada's Japanese community. The Vancouver Asahi became that symbol, the Nikkei heroes of the community.

As for the Asahi themselves, the only thing on their minds was their approaching debut game, and the doggedly intense daily practices. Now the focus returns to the Powell Street Grounds, where the team's bright, energetic voices ring out.

CHAPTER 4

# The Start of a Legend

## Favorable Omens

One day after the usual early morning practice ended, Asahi manager Matsujiro "Harry" Miyasaki called his players over. His face softening momentarily from its usual stoic mask, he said, "You're playing next Sunday. Good news, right?"

"Hurray!"

The eagerly awaited debut game of the Vancouver Asahi was on at last! The players jumped up and down and cheered, hugging each other in an explosion of happiness.

The Asahi team's big goal was to win the championship in a league composed of strong white teams, but there are first steps to take for any goal. Their first opponent would be Mizuho, a Nikkei team made up of workers from a Vancouver sawmill. The Nikkei baseball teams still lacked the strength and ability to play against the dominant white teams, so they had no alternative but to play against each other. Besides, the Asahi was a fledgling team, made up of teenage boys.

There was no reason a veteran white team would play against them.

Playing against other Nikkei teams would help the Asahi players mature and grow stronger. Harry Miyasaki took the rational long view toward reaching their ultimate objective of becoming the number one team.

The Powell Street Grounds were bathed in summer sunshine that Sunday afternoon in July 1914 for the Asahi's debut game. There were no bleachers, so the few hundred spectators simply stood around the field. Most of them were Nikkei living nearby.

The number of people who enjoyed watching the Asahi practice had grown, and the crowd was intrigued. What kind of team was the Asahi? What kind of game would they play?

"But look, they're just kids," said a spectator who'd already made up his mind about the results of the game.

"Hey you, haven't you seen the Asahi practice? They're pretty good," another fan replied.

Soon the teams emerged amid cheers and applause. They lined up on each side of home base and bowed to each other. Then the Asahi took the field. The lineup was as follows:

Teddy Furumoto, Pitcher, #9
Sotaro Matsumiya, Catcher, #7
Yo Horii, First Base, #1
Jim Tabata, Second Base, #8
Tom Matoba, Third Base, #4
Eddy Kitagawa, Shortstop, #3
Ken Suzuki, Right Field, #5
Tony Kodama, Center Field, #6
Mickey Kitagawa, Left Field, #2

"Play ball!" The umpire shouted, and the game was on.

The crowd held its collective breath, waiting for the first pitch. Teddy Furumoto held the ball and glove tight to his chest, checked catcher Sotaro Matsumiya's signal, went into his big windup and flung the ball toward Sotaro's mitt, which was hovering in the strike zone. The ball made a beeline for the mitt as if magnetized. The batter looked down unbelievingly as the ball thumped into the deep leather pocket.

The umpire paused a moment, then raised his arm. "Strike!"

Cheers from the crowd mixed with groans and grunts of surprise from the Mizuho bench. While the first pitch wasn't particularly fast, it was thrown with strength and control, and had deceptive speed. Hard to believe that a young teenager had thrown it, some in the crowd remarked.

The young Asahi battery continued with their aggressive strategy, putting the second pitch right down the middle again. The batter swung hard, his bat passing under the ball and looping up toward the sky. Another strike!

The crowd, expecting a strikeout on the next pitch, craned their necks. The next pitch was high, making the count one ball and two strikes. For the first time, Sotaro shifted his mitt to the outside. Teddy nodded slightly. The ball curved wide and low, under control.

The batter moved forward, but did not swing, his timing thrown off by the unexpected curveball.

"Strike! You're out!" the umpire called, and the crowd cheered.

Another fastball greeted the next batter, and another. He just stared as both pitches came in. Two quick strikes. The battery went for the third strike with another high, straight one, but Teddy had released the ball too early. The batter saw the ball coming right at him and stayed in the box, letting it hit him on the arm.

"Is that how a grown man behaves?" the crowd jeered, and the new baserunner looked down at his feet.

Teddy now had a runner on first and was facing Mizuho's cleanup hitters. Eddy Kitagawa, the shortstop, headed for the pitcher's mound. "Let them hit, Teddy," he said. "We'll take care of things."

The third Mizuho batter took a couple of swings, then stepped into the batter's box, determined to get the first hit. There was no way he would allow a pitcher, talented but a decade younger, make a fool of him.

After checking the first baserunner, Teddy threw one straight down the middle. Expecting another fastball, the batter swung hard but missed. Cheers rose from the crowd again.

A curveball outside and a fastball inside followed. The count was two balls and one strike. The batter swatted at the fourth pitch, a high inside fastball, and popped up for an easy out.

The fourth batter took his stance in the right-hand batter's box. He looked clever and agile, a completely different type than the previous batter, who had relied on sheer power.

Sotaro signed for a high outside curve, figuring it would be too dangerous to tempt this batter with a fastball. But Teddy shook his head. He wanted to test the strength of his signature pitch.

Teddy didn't care about the runner on first at this point, either. He raised both arms in his windup, placed his weight firmly on one leg, and let the ball fly. It was a fastball, a little on the inside. The bat flashed around and just kissed the ball, sending it back foul.

Sotaro knew Teddy's personality, so he was signaling for fastballs now. The next one went wide, but the batter swung and missed. Next, they tempted the batter with a high fastball. It was too high, though, and the batter checked his swing. Now the count was one ball and two strikes.

The deciding pitch was inside and low. There was a solid thwack. The ball flew toward the gap between first and second. Yo Horii, the first baseman, and Jim Tabata, handling second, both headed for it. Jim got to the rolling ball first, scooped it up barehanded, half turned, and tossed it underhand to Teddy, who was already heading to first as backup. He caught the ball and kicked the bag before the batter could get there.

Loud cheers and applause enveloped the field for a long time. The crowd had witnessed the Asahi's first response on defense, a superbly coordinated play rarely seen in grassroots Nikkei baseball. It totally changed how they regarded the team. No one thought the Asahi were "just a kid's team" anymore.

Pitching a mix of fastballs and curveballs, Teddy wasn't giving the Mizuho batters anything to hit. They were swinging late on his fastballs, and their timing was thrown off by the young hurler's artful curveballs. No bat hit a ball squarely.

As the game progressed, however, there was an obvious difference in power between the two teams. There was no doubt that the Asahi offense lacked physical power. After all, they were kids of 14 and 15. Other than Eddy Kitagawa and Tom Matoba, who batted cleanup, the Asahi batters were relatively weak.

The Asahi batters may have been weaker, but they managed to hit balls through the infield, and the cleanup hitters would advance the runners. The Mizuho team's errors, foul balls and hit batters piled up. By the end of the sixth inning, the Asahi had a commanding 15-2 lead. They had given up the two runs on two hits that were Texas Leaguers; bloop singles that plopped down between the infield and the outfield, and a walk combined with an infield error.

It was the top of the seventh inning, and Mizuho had already suffered two outs. The teams had agreed beforehand to call the game if there was a ten-run difference at the bottom of the seventh. The Mizuho squad, so far behind the Asahi, had already lost their will to win.

On the other hand, Teddy's pitches were still steady, with deceptive deadliness. The last batter popped a fly to right field for the final out.

On the mound, Teddy raised his arms in triumph. His teammates quickly surrounded him in a celebratory circle. Coach Miyasaki watched his charges, his arms crossed.

The crowd's excitement did not stop for a long time. More than a few spectators witnessing this spectacular first game began to dream about the Asahi taking on the white baseball teams. That there was a team of kids like this among the Nikkei, a team that could one day meet that challenge, was a revelation. But the Asahi was still a rookie squad that needed experience to smooth out their rough edges. It would take a lot more time for them to develop the signature brand of baseball that would one day seduce their fans.

Coach Miyasaki could clearly see what lay ahead. "These kids will grow stronger still," he told the fans who came to congratulate him. "Their time will come."

The strong summer sunshine still bathed the Powell Street Grounds. For the crowd, reluctant to leave, it was evident that here were intimations of the heroes the Nikkei community had long been waiting and praying for.

## A Very Special Team

In bars, public baths and wherever people gathered, talk of the Asahi beating an adult team spread quickly throughout the Japanese community that day.

People who'd been at the game talked excitedly, while those that missed the action felt disappointed and vowed to see the next one.

The day after the team's debut, the Powell Street Grounds at dawn looked a little different. People surrounded the field, wanting to catch a glimpse of the squad that had become an overnight sensation in Japan Town. For many people in Japan Town, male and female, young and old, it was a pleasure to watch the Asahi team practice.

Meanwhile, invitations to play from various teams rolled in. At that time, in and around Vancouver, many Nikkei teams, such as the Mikado and Yamato, were being established.

The Asahi nine never turned down an invitation to play against anyone, intent on building up their strength and skills. Two years after their debut, they were regarded as the best of the Nikkei teams.

The team's strength was built through intense daily practices much harder than those of any other team. Coach Miyasaki would never relax the reins until they won a championship in a white league. He made sure the team was united in their desire to win, a goal no other Nikkei team pursued with equal fervor. The stronger the Asahi became, the harder the practices got.

None of the players complained. They knew exactly what their mission was, and what was expected of them. As long as time and fate allowed, they never wanted to stop chasing the ball and swinging their bats.

"We just loved baseball," former Asahi player Yuki Uno said many years later. "That was the most important thing."

The reputation of the Asahi even spread to the United States. There, many Nikkei teams had been playing well before teams were formed in Canada. Games with Washington State teams from Seattle and Tacoma, which were not so far from Vancouver, increased. Soon there would be league games made up of teams in the area.

As the Asahi grew stronger, so did the local support from Japan Town. Financial backing for the Asahi came from local stores and businesspeople, who contributed a thousand dollars every year—a considerable sum for the time.

In this way, the Asahi were able to play away games on road trips within British Columbia and to the U.S. West Coast, riding on trains, ships and wagons. Their backers ensured that the team had first-class uniforms and equipment.

Other Nikkei teams operated on a grassroots level. It was obvious that the Asahi were head and shoulders above the rest. The expectations for them were correspondingly bigger: Only a few years after their formation, they were recognized as a star team and a symbol of the Nikkei community. The legend of the Asahi had begun the day of their debut game.

## A Farm System Takes Shape

The Asahi were heroes to the Nikkei children. Any boy who liked baseball dreamed of wearing the Asahi uniform and being a star. It was a glittering alternative to the limited job opportunities then available to the Nikkei.

It wasn't just the boys themselves, either. Many families from all over British Columbia came to Vancouver so their sons could try out for the team. By the team's fourth year, that led to the formation of a five-team farm team system. The Asahi team was at the top, followed by the Cubs. Then came the Athletics, Beavers and Clovers. This structure was unprecedented, and signaled the special status the team had within the Japanese community.

The entire system was extremely competitive, and players had to be outstanding to be picked, and phenomenally talented to advance to the next team above theirs. For a player to advance from the Clovers to the Asahi was an unbelievably hard road. It took Ken Kusutake twenty years. Many players advanced to the Athletics or Cubs but never made the ultimate leap to the Asahi level.

There was no lack of boys trying out for the Asahi. Players selected for the teams automatically got uniforms and gear, and they would race home and immediately try on their uniforms. Many could not sleep from excitement and joy that night.

Even fathers whose young sons made the Clover team were thrilled. More than a few proudly polished the spikes of their sons' shoes every day. The Asahi members were the elite among the elite, heroes among heroes.

The Asahi system was not structured into five teams just because there were so many applicants. It was necessary to create a system that was deep enough to develop players who could compete against the dominant white teams. The system sent outstanding athletes from each level up to the next, which guaranteed that the Asahi always got the best players available. The structure produced excellent results, preparing the Asahi for the tough challenges to come.

## Playing Against White Teams

The Asahi team structure had just been put into place around 1915-1916 when the Vancouver-based International League issued an invitation to join.

Made up of teams of different nationalities, and including both minorities and whites, the International League's level was high, well above the grassroots level, but still below that of the white teams. For the Asahi, who were always looking to compete with outside teams, the invite was a welcome development. If the Asahi could win the International League championship, their higher level of play would be recognized—a big step to open the doors necessary to play against the white teams.

Once the Asahi decided to play in the International League, talk in Japan Town focused on the dream of having a Japanese team compete with the white teams. For the Japanese, who had suffered discrimination for so many years, this was a chance to go head to head for respect. People felt the Asahi would avenge all the heartbreak discrimination had caused if they could win against the white teams.

The International League started their new season in May 1919. The Asahi's first contest was against a team made up of white stevedores who worked on the Vancouver docks.

On game day, the Powell Street Grounds were filled with a sea of spectators. The Nikkei were not the only ones keyed up.

"No matter how good they say they are, they're only a Jap team," white fans were saying. "We'll show them who's the strongest!" The white players and fans were eager to go up against the Asahi, the clear powerhouse among the Nikkei teams.

This was not just a baseball game. For each team, representing white and Japanese society, the game was where prejudice, racism and pride would clash. It was a battlefield. The fans shared the frenzy. The mood at the Powell ballfield was at fever pitch, more than at any Nikkei game.

The Asahi squad was first up to bat. The first batter to step into the pristine batter's box was Yo Horii. Catcalls flew from the white crowd. "Hey, Shorty! Sure you can swing that big bat?"

Yo Horii was one of the shortest players on the Asahi, standing only 150 centimeters tall—less than five feet. The opposing pitcher was well over 180 centimeters. With a physique built up by working on the docks, he looked immense.

"Play ball!" the white umpire shouted.

The ball, thrown at full strength, flew over Yo's head to smash against the back screen. The crowd oohed and aahed.

The second and third pitches went high and wide. The pitcher, apparently rattled by Yo's lack of height, was losing control. He threw another bad pitch, and Yo trotted to first on a walk.

The next batter up was Mickey Kitagawa. Seeing Yo take off for second, Mickey helped out with a long, lazy swing for a strike.

Yo slid, and his momentum carried him to second. He jumped up lightly to stand on the base. The steal was an unqualified success.

The Japanese crowd applauded the textbook-perfect team play between Mickey and Yo. Despite their different last names, Mickey, Eddy and Yo were brothers who had immigrated together, and their quick and instinctive coordination was famous among the Asahi fans.

Mickey hit the third pitch, sending a grounder between third base and shortstop. Yo, who had taken a long lead, raced to third base as the shortstop scrambled for the ball. By the time he'd picked it up, Mickey was closing in on first base. In a panic, the shortstop overthrew, and the first baseman fumbled the ball. At the end of the play, Yo had scored the first run, and Mickey was standing on second with his arms crossed. It was the Asahi's first incredibly speedy attack. The pitcher's face was an angry red at the unexpected run.

Next up was Eddy, the last of the three Kitagawa brothers. The white team's strategy, which was to overpower the Asahi physically, was backfiring. The next pitch was thrown with overconfident strength, and ended up being an easy target for Eddy. He stroked the ball into shallow centerfield. Runners were on first and third.

Tom Matoba was up next. Soon to be known as the "Japanese Babe Ruth," Tom was short but very stocky and powerful. He was a slugger, unusual among the Nikkei players.

"Hit 'em with your best shot, Tom!"

With the cheers of the Nikkei crowd behind him, Tom stepped into the batter's box. After fouling one pitch off and taking two balls, he slugged the fourth pitch, a liner that divided left field neatly in two and disappeared into the standing-room-only crowd surrounding the fenceless field.

Mickey and Eddy raced home. The ball, lost in the crowd, was not found easily. Tom, powerful but slow on the basepaths, reached third base. The umpire, however, called it a ground-rule double, and Tom was sent back to second.

The Nikkei crowd jeered and booed.

"Cheat! Fire the umpire!"

Helped by their opponents' errors, the Asahi turned two singles into two more runs for a total of five runs. It was a brilliant league debut.

The white team's offense was rough and ready. Seemingly without a strategy, each batter simply swung for the fences. All of the players looked powerful enough to hit the ball over the horizon, but that would only happen if they could make solid contact—and that wasn't happening.

On the mound again for the Asahi stood Teddy Furumoto, the team's ace. Teddy's arsenal of fastballs, knucklers, curves and an "indrop"—a curveball that drops—stopped the big men in their tracks during their at-bats in the bottom of the first inning.

During the second inning, the white team tried to catch a ground ball hit by an Asahi player. The pitcher, running to help, kicked the ball with his spikes. Meanwhile, the young Asahi player ran home. Even the white fans could do nothing but laugh at that point.

The preconception that the Asahi was an easy team to beat was undergoing a sea change. The white fans had never witnessed this kind of quick, intelligent play from any other Nikkei team. Compared to their opponents, the Asahi were superb defensively and offensively. When Yo stepped into the batter's box for the third time, someone yelled "Hey Shorty! Go for it!"

Surprisingly, the cheer was from a white fan. Did he have enough faith in his team to be able to cheer for the other side? Had he lost faith in his bumbling team? Or had he been seduced by the Asahi's dazzling performance? Quite a few white fans were cheering for the Asahi by that point.

The players on the Asahi team, 14 and 15 years old when the team was formed, were in their early twenties now.

One of the original members of the Asahi, Teddy Furumoto, had developed into a multitalented player, capable of serving as pitcher, shortstop or right fielder. The entire team had endured hours of long practices and played incessantly. The five-team farm structure also gave them an unprecedented depth of talent at every position. There was no other team in the International League like the Asahi.

In the sixth inning, the one black player on the white team hit a two-run home run. Teddy had walked the previous batter, and was distracted. A powerful swing sent his first pitch rocketing toward left field, across Jackson Avenue and onto the roof of a house.

Teddy glanced over at Mickey Kitagawa in left field, who was waving goodbye to the ball. "That pitch was too direct," Teddy murmured to himself. He felt strangely refreshed as he watched the ball disappear into the blue sky. Anyway, the Asahi still had a huge lead, 12-2, so the situation wasn't as bad as it could have been.

As the game entered the ninth inning, Teddy had allowed just four hits, including the one by the runner now on first.

The batter hit a dribbler toward second base. Yuji Uchimura at second easily scooped up the ball, throwing it to shortstop Eddy Kitagawa, who quickly tossed it to Yo Horii on first. It was a text-book 4-6-3 double play. The game was over!

Yells and screams of joy from the Nikkei spectators rocked the Powell Street Grounds. They had done it—outplayed a white team! The dream of the Nikkei fans had become reality. Some in the crowd were overcome with tears.

In comparison, the Asahi players were calm. This game had provided a measure of their strength. They'd confirmed their belief and confidence in themselves. After congratulating each other, they were already looking ahead to their next objective.

For the white baseball fans that had witnessed the Asahi play for the first time, the afternoon was a series of surprises. They'd never seen baseball played like that before. It made the hearts of true baseball fans dance.

That night turned into an endless celebration in Japan Town. The people seemed drunk with the pure delight taken in their heroes' deeds.

**CHAPTER 5**

# Small Players, Big Baseball

## The Terminal League Wars

By 1919, the Asahi had shown their potential by conquering the International League and attracting huge crowds.

The team was naturally proud of their first league championship, but the white teams belonging to the International League were weaker than the veteran white teams. The Asahi players wanted to compete in a more powerful league, and they were confident that they were strong enough to do so.

A while after the end of that first championship season, the Terminal League—considered the strongest amateur league on the Canadian west coast—issued an invitation to join the league roster. The Asahi players were more than ready.

The caliber of play in the Terminal League was far higher than the International League, readily evident in the types of teams the league boasted. Club teams representing the Canadian Pacific Railway Company, the British Columbia Electric Power Company, and

Hudson Bay—a major retail enterprise—were all members. Prominent local companies, such as hotels and newspapers, also fielded their own teams. The Terminal League was comparable to the elite modern Japanese corporate team leagues, where power is measured not just on the field but also in corporate prestige.

The Asahi would be on the same field with these heavy hitters, and the team and their Nikkei supporters couldn't have been more delighted at the opportunity.

The Terminal League leadership had made its own calculations before inviting the Asahi. If the Asahi joined the league, they would bring legions of Nikkei spectators with them. The prospect of the strongest Nikkei team battling a top white club team over the championship would attract huge paying audiences of both Nikkei and white fans and radically boost the league's profile. It was proof of the Asahi's ability as well as white society's interest in them.

The Vancouver Asahi joined the Terminal League in 1920, the first Nikkei team ever to do so. It was time to pit Japan Town's pride against the best of the white teams. In the sixth year since their inception, the objective of the Asahi was close at hand.

### A Dull Season and Internal Strife

Baseball season in Vancouver began in May and was over by the beginning of September at the latest. League games were held at various fields around the city. Practice games, exhibition games and away games were held in the off-season after the league games ended, very similar to what happens in the United States and Japan.

Spring is the most invigorating time of year in Vancouver. The flowers begin to bloom, the spring salmon are battling upriver, and the new baseball season starts. In May 1920, Nikkei baseball fans in Vancouver had a special reason for being impatient: the Vancouver Asahi were ready to begin their challenge in the Terminal League.

Crowds of Nikkei thronged to the Powell Street Grounds on the Asahi's game days. Many white baseball fans that had heard of the team also appeared. The presence of the Asahi virtually guaranteed the league organizers a rise in the popularity of the league.

But in contrast to the high expectations, the Asahi's results were unimpressive, and their play featured little of the fast teamwork that had previously captured the hearts of fans. That first season found the Asahi down in fifth place out of just eight Terminal League teams. The Asahi players, their manager, and the Nikkei fans could not hide their disappointment.

What was behind the poor results? For one thing, the club was plagued with internal conflict, which became apparent that autumn just before the season ended. In 1921, manager Bariki Kasahara and five players defected to start a new team, the Tigers, and the Asahi failed to improve their ranking during their second season in the league. As soon as the season finished, they left for Japan to play a series of exhibition games under the guidance of Dr. Seitaro No-mura. Their embarrassing loss to the Wakayama Junior High School team there caused a storm of media criticism. The Asahi, who had enjoyed the momentum of continued success, were up against the wall for the first time in their history.

## A Manager Among Managers—Harry Miyasaki

The effects of the player defection and the unexpected slump in the Terminal League showed that there was an urgent need to rebuild the team, although the hopes and support of Asahi fans remained undiminished.

It was up to Harry Miyasaki, who would become the team's third manager, to rebuild the squad and put them back on track.

Harry had actually been one of the five players who defected, but he could not bear to see what was happening to the Asahi and returned to do something about it. When the team got back from

Japan, Harry and the other four defectors rejoined the squad.

Harry believed it would be difficult to compete in the Terminal League if the Asahi did not evolve. To him, the style of baseball the Asahi played was too straightforward. It was easy to produce a certain level of results with gifted players and hard practice, but that would only make a difference in games against weaker teams.

In the highly competitive Terminal League, it clearly wasn't enough. The Terminal teams were bigger and stronger than the Asahi, so the key for the team was to formulate their own brand of winning baseball. Otherwise, Harry was convinced, it would be impossible for them to win the league championship.

The players who had not defected and played the exhibition games in Japan had had the opportunity to assess their playing form against Wakayama Junior High School, which had won the famed Koshien tournament.

Koshien was where the powerhouse teams of Japan's junior high school baseball system competed—a showcase for the nation's most talented players in an age without professional baseball teams or even the Tokyo Big Six University League. Wakayama won the first of two successive championships in the Koshien university association that summer.

Eiji Sawamura and Victor Starfin, both talented pitchers in the tournament, later dropped out of the school baseball system to join the Japan All-Stars. Sawamura would become one of Japan's legendary pitchers, and Starfin would go on to be "Japan's favorite blue-eyed pitcher." When the two left school in 1934, they were 16 and 17 years old, respectively. As members of the Japan All-Stars, they competed in exhibition matches against the Major League All-Stars, featuring Babe Ruth and Lou Gehrig, during their Japan tour.

The Wakayama team trained a great deal to accomplish their precision plays. Firm defense was at the core, and on offense the goal was to advance at least one base. The team also had an impressive offense that efficiently stitched together skillful sacrifice hits, bunts, hit-and-run plays, and stolen bases to fit specific scenario. It was the essence of Japanese baseball, which endures to this day. This strategy ensured that all efforts were focused on scoring the first run.

The Asahi had leapt to prominence in Vancouver by playing precisely that kind of baseball—a typically Japanese style of play that it had never come across in Vancouver's league games. However, compared to the polished Wakayama school team, the Asahi were still playing too instinctively—not a winning formula in the tough Terminal League. The Wakayama school team was miles ahead of the Asahi in terms of understanding and implementing strategy, the level of each player's understanding of roles and cooperation in team play, as well as the quality and experience in working each play.

However, the players of both Wakayama Junior High School and the Vancouver Asahi were the same—Japanese. From this defeat, the Asahi gained an important insight into how to break out of their Terminal League slump.

The players who had remained to play the Japan exhibition tour and those who had defected came to the same conclusion: Harry was the perfect man for the job of rebuilding the Asahi. As manager, he paid attention to details of how best to restructure the team and its style of play, and he was said to be even more zealous than the club's founding manager, Matsujiro Miyazaki.

Harry would carve out time from managing a dry cleaning business to spend as much time as possible with the Asahi. Not only did he deal with over a hundred games per year and daily practices, he also gave rides to players who needed them and worked with injured players as well. Harry expended an enormous amount of energy on the team.

At the time, for example, chicken eggs were expensive and difficult to obtain. Before important games, Harry would buy as many eggs as he could to make *tamago gohan*—rice with eggs—which he would have his players eat for stamina before the game.

Everyone who knew the Asahi immediately thought of Harry as the team's new manager. People called him "Manager among Managers." Though part of the team had once seceded, he did not force any confrontations.

Instead, Harry was consumed by the question of how to revamp and reenergize his squad. How can I strengthen the Asahi? He wondered. How can I make the team strong enough to compete against the best white teams when we're physically smaller?

Harry laid the foundation of his team remodeling upon the strategic use of the best Nikkei traits and characteristics: cooperation, deftness, quickness, intelligence and diligence would be the tools deployed to establish a new, original and winning Asahi style.

The first thing to do, he believed, was to strengthen the defense. Next was to concentrate on bunting, stealing bases, the hit-and-run or run-and-hit, and going for sacrifice flies to keep runners moving toward home for the win. The Asahi needed to have a logical playing style that could fit any situation. This was the style of the Wakayama team to which the Asahi had lost, and it is very similar to the "small ball" style that has become the focus of interest in Major League Baseball.

## Japanese Spirit and Fair Play

It wasn't just strategy and skills that Harry wanted to impart to his players, either.

The Asahi must win, he thought, but it isn't enough just to win.

Previously there had been no goal for the Asahi other than to defeat the dominant white teams. During a time of anti-Japanese discrimination and boycotts, a win against those clubs was a vote of confidence and a source of pride for the Nikkei. Victory was the supreme order of the day, but by Harry's standards that did not mean the end justified the means. Baseball was not just an arena where victory or defeat against white society was measured. The Nikkei should be able to enjoy a confidence-building victory from the bottom of their hearts. A baseball diamond was one of the rare places where real communication between the white and Japanese communities was possible.

It therefore made sense to avoid trouble. Harry did not want to play a game in which the reputation of the Nikkei would be needlessly damaged and confirm white prejudices and preconceptions about the Japanese.

Harry gathered the players together to address them.

"No matter what happens, do not play a shameful game," he advised. "We are Japanese. Do not forget the true spirit of the Japanese or the spirit of the samurai. Chivalry is the rule."

For the Nikkei, who had left their homeland to make new lives in Canada, retaining the spirit of Japanese chivalry was integral to their identity and pride. Whether facing the discrimination of a seemingly superior white society, or physically confronting a rioting white mob, the mantra of "true Japanese spirit" in their hearts helped construct a mental fortress that, in turn, overcame barriers and even true physical danger.

For example, Harry absolutely forbade his players to protest to the umpires about any rough play. Once the players trotted onto the field, their responsibility was to "play bravely, resolutely, fair and square."

From the Nikkei crowd, cheers of *"Yamato damashi!"* and *"Bushido seishin!"* could often be heard at Asahi games. One day, a curious white spectator asked a Nikkei fan, "What do those cheers mean, anyway?"

The Nikkei fan thought it difficult to explain, but he attempted a translation.

"Well, *yamato damashi* means the spirit of fair play, and *bushido seishin* stands for sportsmanship," he replied.

Every day in preparation for the upcoming season, the Asahi went through strenuous practice sessions. Offensive and defensive set plays, bunting, base stealing, and other field tactics were practiced endlessly.

At long last, the rainy season ended, and spring came to Vancouver. Harry Miyasaki and a newly spirited Asahi were ready for another challenge in the Terminal League.

## The Birth of "Brain Ball"

May 1922: The third season for the Asahi in the Terminal League was about to begin, and the true worth of the Asahi team and Harry Miyasaki would be tested. The Asahi had followed Harry's leadership and made a new style of play all their own. There was nothing left but to produce results.

It took very little time for the fans and the other teams to notice the change. It became apparent during the second game of the season, against the Canadian Pacific Railway team.

The opposing pitcher was not at his best in the early innings, and the Asahi took advantage by scoring three quick runs. However, behind a spirited offense, the CPR team came from behind in the sixth inning to take a 5-3 lead.

The opposing pitcher had got his groove back. He began to throw heavy pitches, and the Asahi batters could barely hit the ball to the infield. It seemed impossible for the Asahi to mount any kind of scoring threat. The game was turning out to be a typical example of Asahi losses during the past two seasons. The Nikkei fans felt that the Asahi had to find a way to throw off the opposing team's dominance.

When the Asahi were losing mid-game, they were too weak offensively to come from behind. Moreover, they would allow the opposing team to score more runs. The batters on the white teams were able to take advantage of their physical strength to hit and score, while the Asahi could not.

This time, however, the Asahi were about to prove they were a notch above the level they'd reached the previous two seasons. In the bottom of the seventh, Harry gave them his instructions.

The first batter hit a safety bunt toward third. The next batter followed Harry's sign for a push bunt—a run and bunt—and swiftly switched his stance to do so. The opposing pitcher's motion was easy to read. As the pitcher raised his leg for the windup, the runner on first started his steal. The second baseman crouched, ready for the ball to come his way. The bunted ball squirted between first and second, and now runners were on first and second.

The third batter also bunted. This time it was clearly a sacrifice play to advance the runners. The third baseman fielded the bunt, throwing the batter out, putting runners on second and third.

The crowd was agape at the bunt offensive, clearly wondering what was going on. The opposing team, both on the field and in the dugout, began to lose their composure.

And now the fourth batter was up. There were two strategies possible: a squeeze play or a hit to score a run. The count went to two balls and one strike. The batter confirmed Harry's signal, and returned to the batter's box.

As the pitcher started his windup, the runners on second and third took off. The batter swung, sending the ball rolling between short and third. It was a squeeze bunt that effectively stopped the ball's momentum.

The runner on third ran full tilt toward home. The third baseman scooped up the ball and threw it home. By the time the ball reached the catcher, however, the runner had slid home, his foot kissing home plate. The catcher, not even imagining that the second runner would keep going, automatically threw to first.

Harry's strategy was not a squeeze play to get one run. The runner on second had orders to run at full speed for home plate, not stopping safely at third as he would in a normal squeeze situation. The catcher's throw to first glanced off the first baseman's glove, and the ball rolled into the outfield. The second runner charged home, followed by the batter.

A single bunt, and the batter and runners on the diamond had all scored. The crowd went wild.

The Asahi had always included bunting in their offensive strategy, but this was the first time they had hit four successive bunts. The intentional bunt attack shocked the opposing team and completely changed the flow of the game. The physically bigger CPR team was slow and awkward in response to the Asahi's quick, efficient, precision play.

Harry later gave the signal for a hit-and-run. The ball rolled between the shortstop and third base. Another run was on the board, and the Asahi had come from behind to take a 7-5 lead.

Harry's strategy was based on logic, and could be applied rationally to any situation. He was supremely confident in its effectiveness.

With another runner perched on first again, the next batter up bunted to advance him. Now the runner was on second, with two outs. The always-reliable Tom Matoba smacked a timely hit, and the score was now 8-5. The Asahi had gained five runs in the inning, and they were on a roll. The Nikkei crowd cheered them on.

The CPR team was in a state of shock in the face of this sudden and unexpected turnabout. Staked to a three-run lead, Teddy Furumoto regained his usual deadly form. The defense was coolly efficient. They succeeded in keeping CPR at bay for the next two innings.

The moment the game ended, the Nikkei crowd erupted in a frenzy. They had endured the disappointing results of the past couple of seasons to finally see the Asahi back in form. The victory was an exhilarating example that confirmed the Asahi style of play.

At some point, Harry's strategy became known as "brain ball." To put it plainly, it was playing baseball as a thinking man's game.

## Kamikaze Baseball

During the third season of Harry's tenure, the Asahi showed off their new playing style and finished third in the Terminal League standings, beating a number of experienced teams. The team had proven to themselves that going for the league title was not an impossible dream.

From early summer, the days grew longer and longer until you might wonder when darkness would fall in Vancouver. Children ran home from school to do household chores and earn the 10 cents that would pay for a ticket, and then hurry with their parents and other adults to the ball field. On the days the Asahi played, such scenes were commonplace. Asahi games always drew a full house.

The Nikkei population in the area at that time totaled around ten thousand people. It's said that when a pennant game was being played fully half of the Japanese population living in Vancouver would crowd the Powell Street Grounds, leaving the streets of Japan Town silent and empty.

Whether the Asahi had won or lost, Japan Town would inevitably be in chaos after the game as spectators flowed from the ball field to the streets. Trains and cars would come to a standstill until the waves of people finally ebbed.

The Asahi's popularity was not limited to the Nikkei anymore, either. They stood out among the power-based teams with their quick and strategic playing style, which appealed to the entire crowd. The Asahi offense was constantly evolving.

In one game, the Asahi faced a highly regarded pitcher of professional caliber. It was apparent that any attempt to meet his pitches head-on would be a losing proposition. So the Asahi bunted, from the first pitch to the last. This was their forte.

"Drop it!" The Asahi would call out from the bench, putting pressure on their opponent. The Asahi used the word *drop* to mean bunt.

The constant bunting meant that the opposing defenders had to keep running and moving. This had the same effect as body blows, tiring out opponents so that eventually they would make errors. Taking advantage of the errors and walks, the Asahi would finally make a squeeze play to score a run.

As a result, the Asahi won the game with no hits. All the runs were earned on squeeze plays. "Very few pitchers who throw a no-hitter lose the game," a newspaper sarcastically commented on the game the next day, "but the pitcher who faced the Vancouver Asahi last night did."

In a different game, the Asahi won by fearlessly continuing to steal bases. With two out and runners on first and second, for example, the Asahi put on a double steal, knowing the opposing team would assume that no one would steal with two outs.

The catcher, realizing he would never make the throw to third in time, threw to second instead. The second baseman, seeing the runner rounding third for home, threw the ball back to the catcher. But the runner made it home safely. In the meantime, the runner on first was about to round second for third. The defense panicked, taken aback at the audacity and sheer speed of the Asahi. The balls thrown to second and third were seconds behind the first baserunner, who made it home. Two runs scored without a single hit.

Depending on the opposing pitcher, the Asahi were able to bat their way to a victory as well.

Opposing teams naturally studied the Asahi, who were racking up wins in spectacular fashion. And at times the bigger white teams would play rough in their attempts to keep the Asahi from scoring. The Asahi team, trained well by Harry, never retaliated or attempted any rough play themselves. The Asahi's fair play could never be called into question.

In time, Nikkei fans would say, "Harry Miyasaki didn't just rebuild the Asahi into a winning team. He raised the Asahi players into responsible, upstanding Canadian citizens." It was no surprise that white society realized what kind of values the Asahi exemplified, and ultimately supported the team.

Some white fans would cheer when the Asahi were on defense with a runner on first, calling out "Double play! Double play!" They wanted to see one of the picture-perfect double plays the Asahi could turn, said by some to be more beautiful than any in the majors.

Other whites in the crowd would confront the white fans that wanted to see an Asahi double play. "You cheering the Japs?"

"Shut up!" the fans snapped back.

The Nikkei could not help laughing at the situation. It was a source of pride for them that white fans would be fighting over the Asahi. Before anyone realized what was happening, both white and Nikkei fans were chanting "Double play! Double play!"

As a game got into the latter innings, or when it seemed the time had come for the Asahi to make a decisive play, fans among the Nikkei crowd would start saying, "The kamikaze wind will start blowing soon."

To white fans, the Asahi style of play seemed magical. To the Nikkei, the Asahi turned the impossible into the possible. To Harry, making it look easy was the result of careful calculation, hard work and application.

## Sweet Victory at Last

In 1926, six years after joining the Terminal League and twelve years after the team was born, the Asahi were finally in sight of their first league title.

That season, ace Teddy Furumoto and another pitcher, Joe Tanaka, had taken turns on the mound as the Asahi fought for first place. Joe was unusual in that he was a one-armed athlete. His day job was at a sawmill, and one day during the middle of the season his left arm got caught in the conveyor belt and was torn off.

After his accident, Joe initially gave up the idea of ever playing baseball again. Since his right arm was his throwing arm, however, a comeback seemed possible for a determined man like Joe. He trained and trained until he was ready to pitch for the Asahi once more.

Teddy's main weapons were a fastball and a curve. In comparison, Joe would befuddle the batters with his slow curveball. For batters, a slow curve looked like an easy target. So easy, in fact, that they couldn't wait to swat at the tempting ball. They missed more often than not, and this was Joe's most effective weapon.

Joe's fielding was also magnificent. Since he only had one hand, he didn't wear a glove. No matter how hard the ball that came his way was hit, Joe would catch it barehanded and make his throw. He was the most extraordinary player on the field.

In mid-August, victory for the Asahi laid in wait three games ahead. If they won the next game, however, the championship would be theirs. That was because their next game was with the British Columbia Electric company team, currently in second place. It would be their last direct confrontation with the BC team.

If the Asahi lost, though, they would need to win two more to take the pennant. The Nikkei fans wanted to see more of the Asahi, so they were torn between the two possibilities.

As for the BC team, they faced the dire prospect of allowing a Nikkei team to win the championship for the first time. Besides, they needed a victory to remain in contention for the title. The upcoming game was the talk of Vancouver.

Game day. The crowd began to arrive hours before the first pitch, and soon the Powell Street Grounds were completely filled. For the Nikkei this was a special game. The Asahi were about to become the new champions of a white league. There was no way any Nikkei fan would miss witnessing such a long-awaited dream about to come true. There was no end to the number of Nikkei fans, the late arrivals elbowing their way into the packed crowd.

Warmup time for both teams ended, and the cheering grew louder in anticipation. Just as the cheering reached its peak, as if it had been planned, the umpire called, "Play ball!"

Harry was determined to win the game and the pennant today. Joe Tanaka was set to pitch first, and Teddy would take the mound for the second half of the contest.

Unlike now, back then there were no mid-game pitchers or relievers. It was normal for one pitcher to work the entire game. Once he took the mound, almost nothing would get him to give it up. Teddy was that kind of pitcher.

For this all-important game, however, Harry chose to use both his aces. Though this strategy was unusual, it was indicative of how much Harry wanted to win. He had faith in young Joe, who had shown his incredible willpower during his comeback from serious injury. He also believed in Teddy, who displayed a cool steadiness and simply refused to lose.

Both Joe and the BC batters were stiff with tension as the crucial game began, their timing and rhythm visibly off. Joe could not relax into his usual effective pitching style, and the BC hitters were swinging away freely but mostly producing pop flies that the Asahi defense snagged. The Asahi offensive engine didn't roar to life immediately, either. The BC team, which could not afford to drop this game, had sent their top pitcher to the mound. A contender for the season's pitching award, he could throw fast and hard.

The Asahi went for their tried and tested bunt strategy, but the defense was ready. Though Asahi runners would get on base occasionally, they were stopped from scoring.

After BC's batters had gone through their entire lineup once, Harry sensed that they'd taken Joe's measure. Now his problem was whether to relieve Joe and send in Teddy, or leave Joe in to keep battling.

A heavy, tense atmosphere enveloped the field. The BC team was the first to break the scoreless impasse. As Harry predicted, BC's batters had gotten the timing of Joe's pitches down. At the top of the fourth, the first batter hit a line drive between left and center and reached second. The next batter got another double. One run was on the board for the powerful company team.

The next batter hit a ball toward second but the ball was caught, with the runner on second advancing to third base. The count was three balls and one strike for the next batter, who hit Joe's next slow curveball into the narrow gap between third and short. Another run scored, making it 2-0 with a man on first.

"Relax, Joe, relax," the Asahi defense and bench called out to their pitcher.

Joe couldn't control his panic. After he walked the next batter, Harry found himself calling time out and trotting to the mound. After saying just a few quiet words to Joe, though, he returned to the bench. It was too soon to switch to Teddy, and Harry could only hope that Joe would stop the assault.

Play resumed. One out, runners on first and second. Thinking of the BC pitcher, the Asahi couldn't afford to give up any more runs.

On the third pitch to the next batter, however, it was as if the hitter was waiting for the high fastball Joe threw. He drove a low grasscutter toward left field. The Nikkei crowd groaned. But just when it looked as if the ball would make it through, shortstop Teddy Furumoto dove and caught it in his outstretched glove. Scrambling to one knee, he twisted his body and threw the ball to second—the kind of acrobatic fielding that was Teddy's forte.

The runner on second had broken for third, figuring there was no way the ball would be caught. He tried to return to base but was tagged out. The ball was swiftly thrown to first for a double play. The Asahi had prevented the third additional run they feared.

Teddy was the key to stopping the BC assault that inning. The Asahi squad had fewer players than the other teams, so each Asahi player was trained to play several positions. When he was not on the mound, pitching ace Furumoto could be found at shortstop or patrolling right field. In this game, Teddy was the shortstop until he was called to the mound.

The Asahi were able to relax after the unexpected double play. They were back on form. In the bottom of the fourth, the Asahi assault began with the third batter in the lineup, Tom Miyata. Along with Tom Matoba, who batted fourth, he was known as a slugger.

Tom hit the third pitch toward left field. The ball landed in fair territory and then bounded foul. The Nikkei crowd on the third base line headed wordlessly toward the field to narrow the space and make it harder for the BC defenders to move freely.

Whether that strategy was effective or not, Tom Miyata made it to second base easily. Tom Matoba was walked, putting the potential tying run on base. The next Asahi batter hit a sacrifice fly, advancing both runners. One out, with men on second and third.

Determined not to lose his lead, the BC pitcher threw his best fastball. Ken Yamamura, batting sixth, could only respond with a weak dribbler back to the mound and was thrown out. Two out, runners still on second and third.

The next batter was the best bunter on the team, Frank Nakamura. His technique was so good, in fact, that it didn't matter how many outs there were. Frank was capable of bunting the ball wherever he wanted.

Frank had never hit a double, much less a home run. And even with two outs, it was still possible to go for a safety bunt. The BC defense had dealt with Frank's bunting before, though, and in anticipation of the expected ploy the infielders had drawn in close. If the ball went between or over them, that would be their bad luck.

The count was two balls and one strike. Frank stood in a bunting stance in the batter's box. But the defense was so tight and prepared for a bunt that it would be risky for even Frank to try one, so Harry had given him the sign to swing away. On the next pitch, Nakamura suddenly switched to a regular hitting stance and swung hard.

The ball headed for the pitcher, caromed off the edge of his glove and bounded toward second. In the meantime, the runner on third reached home. Frank was safe at first.

The crowd alternatively held its breath or cheered at the risky play.

Two outs, runners on first and third. Teddy Furumoto, batting eighth in the lineup, was at the plate. Teddy was an excellent pitcher and loved to throw, but he liked batting, too. He was known for his control at bat, able to spray line drives to the left or right. When he was not pitching, his batting had saved the day many times before. In all his time with the Asahi, though, he'd never clouted a home run.

The opposing team knew Teddy was a polished hitter, and were not taking him lightly. The defense was keyed up, and so was Teddy.

The next batter up is Joe, Teddy thought. It would be difficult to rely on him. It's up to me.

There was no choice but to hit away, and everyone on the field, in the dugouts and the crowd knew it.

The first pitch was a ball, low and outside. Teddy swung. He needed to make a hit. Strike one. He stepped out of the box and swung the bat a couple of times, then looked to the bench. He slowly returned to the batter's box. He raised his bat high and waited, relaxed.

The catcher and pitcher were convinced they had the advantage. As the pitcher raised his arms and began his a powerful windup, the Asahi runner on third broke for home. Teddy brought his bat low and toward his chest. He was going for a squeeze bunt!

The crowd's shock quickly turned to anticipation. The ball rolled toward third. Caught flatfooted, the third baseman was slow off the mark. It was impossible to stop the runner on third from scoring, but he could still throw Teddy out. He hustled to pick up the ball but couldn't get his glove on it.

Teddy steamed into first, and Frank was safe on third. The Asahi had turned a problematic two-out situation into a 2-2 tie, and had two men on base!

Now it was time to do or die. After a quiet word with Joe, Harry approached the umpire with the name of the pinch hitter. Harry was putting all his money and hopes on the next batter, Roy Yamamura.

Roy was to become one of the most popular Asahi players ever, but at that time he was only a fourth-year player. At just 150 centimeters, he was also among the shortest players on the squad, but his athletic ability and hitting prowess were unmatched.

The BC pitcher changed his strategy, throwing curves instead of straight pitches. Roy fouled off the potential strikes and resisted swinging at the balls outside the strike zone, though, running the count to two balls and two strikes.

The seventh pitch was a big curving sinker. Roy's half-swing sent the ball hopping toward first, where it flew over the first baseman's glove into right field.

The Asahi had come from behind to take a 3-2 lead! The team and the crowd were convinced that today was the day they would take the long-awaited championship.

Standing on the rubber after replacing Joe Tanaka, Teddy was a fish in water. He was always happiest on the mound, and was feeling especially good after a great defensive play. He knew he had speed and his control was excellent. If it were possible, he would have loved to pitch every day.

Leave it to me, fellas, he thought. Teddy quickly stopped three batters in a row.

With strong pitching by both teams, however, the score remained at 3-2 until the seventh inning. Teddy was facing the BC club's leadoff batter, who stubbornly held on for ten pitches before Teddy threw a sinker low and outside and struck him out.

Teddy relaxed a bit too much, and the next batter hit a line drive single to right. One out, with a runner on base. Now he was up against the heart of the BC order. With the runner on first, the Nikkei fans chanted, "Double play! Double play!" Teddy tensed up, and pitched a little too carefully to walk the batter. One down, runners on first and second.

The next batter was huge, a hulking presence that put pressure on the Asahi battery. Teddy's first pitch was a breaking ball. The batter let it go by. He looked like he was going to ignore everything but a fastball. OK, if that's how you want to play it, Teddy thought, and threw another breaking ball. It was a sweet curve toward center that the BC batter also chose to ignore.

Catcher Reggie Yasui signaled for another curveball, this time to the outside corner. But Teddy shook his head, indicating that he wanted to throw a fastball. The batter would not be expecting the challenge, and Teddy wanted to outthink as well as outpitch the opposition. Considering the lineup for the upcoming innings, this would also be the only chance for Teddy to go up against the league's best slugger.

It was typical of the strong-willed Teddy. He threw a straight fastball a little to the inside. Teddy regretted it as the bat hit the ball with a solid thunk. The ball flew to centerfield, and the only saving grace was that it was too low to be a home run.

The runner on second raced home, and the score was now even, 3-3, with runners on second and third. The fifth batter in the BC lineup was a slugger as well. Teddy couldn't shake his regret regarding the previous pitch. He threw a curve, and it was slammed for a three-run homer.

The British Columbia Electric team and its fans roared back to life. Teddy struck out the two remaining batters to end the inning, but he'd handed the other team a 6-3 come-from-behind lead.

To the Asahi and their dedicated supporters, though, all was not lost. The next inning will be our turn, they said. The Nikkei crowd kept cheering.

The BC team went hitless in the top of the eighth. Now it was the Asahi's chance to mount a comeback. It was time for them to start playing like the Asahi again.

Tom Miyata, first up, got a hit to left field. Tom Matoba grounded out to second, and then Reggie Yasui hit a fly to right for an out. Ken Yamamura and Frank Nakamura, sixth and seventh in the lineup, kept the inning alive with perfect bunts. Now the bases were loaded, but with two outs. Teddy Furumoto, who'd orchestrated the squeeze bunt in the fourth inning, had a chance to work his magic again. I let the other team score because I wasn't concentrating, Teddy thought.

I've got to use my bat to pay the team back for my mistake in letting the BC score. I can't miss.

The pressure was on, but he felt strangely calm. I know my pitching is good, he thought. I just let my focus slip in the seventh. Concentrate. We made the double play and I can't believe we got the perfect squeeze bunt.

He could see that the other team was preparing to defend against another squeeze play. But it didn't matter what kind of defense they were setting up. Don't think of anything outside of hitting the ball as hard as you can, he told himself.

Teddy held the bat loosely, and without thinking, he swung on the count of three, the bat feeling light and coming around in a perfect arc for a chest-high ball. There was a dry thwack as it connected with the ball and sent it flying to left.

The Nikkei on the edge of left field were willing a home run. Come on, come on. They got their wish, and there were wild cheers as the ball sailed over the crowd and disappeared into the standing-room-only section. A grand slam—unbelievable! Teddy thought. As he ran around the bases, he kept his game face on. When he neared the Asahi waiting for him at home plate, though, he smiled for the first time.

It was the first and last home run that Teddy would ever hit for the Asahi. It was a hammer blow to the BC club, putting the Asahi back on top.

In the top of the ninth, Teddy had a one-run lead to protect. He quickly regained the cool rationality needed to finish off the game as the ace.

Faced with the stark possibility that they might lose both the game and the championship, the British Columbia Electric players were going all out to preserve their reputation and pride. Their number two batter was up first. Taking a page from the Asahi playbook, he tapped a safety bunt down the third-base line. Knowing he would never make the play, Tom Matoba gave up throwing to first.

No outs, a runner on first. The next batter was the one who had delivered the huge hit to left center off Joe Tanaka. The time was ripe for a double play, and the Asahi took up their defensive positions.

Teddy continued to pitch with care. But the batter was even more cautious. Unlike before, he was careful not to swing at just any pitch. Teddy's first pitch was a ball, and so were the next three.

Now he had two runners to worry about, but Teddy remained calm and confident on the mound. The difference between a ball and a strike is a mere hairsbreadth. His ball direction was good, his curve under control. He had plenty of stamina since he had only been pitching since the fifth inning.

He was going to face the fourth and fifth batters, who'd scored the BC comeback runs. What was the Asahi going to do? The answer was to go on the attack.

Catcher Reggie Yasui came to the mound and spoke briefly with Teddy. They agreed to concentrate on inside pitches to set up the double play. But inside pitches were dangerous. If the ball was not thrown at precisely the right angle, it could be tagged for an easy hit, even a home run. Teddy held the possibility for heaven or hell in his hands with every pitch.

As Teddy released the ball, it would look like an easy-to-hit inside pitch, but would break sharply inside, cramping the batter's swing. His first and second pitches did just that, heading for the inside corner of the plate.

The first pitch produced a swing and a miss. The second made the batter hit a foul down near his feet. The pressure was on the batter now, and unless Teddy starting making mistakes, the game was in hand.

The third pitch was straight and a bit high. Batter in the hole; he had to swing if the pitch was not an obvious ball. The batter escaped with a foul tip. The field was filled with the crowd's huge sigh.

The battery was still relaxed. It was time to set up the double play. Reggie held his mitt outside and low. Teddy fired a controlled ball that would drop to the target. The batter, standing with his hip set back in anticipation of another inside pitch, could not properly judge the breaking ball coming at him.

He held his swing and watched the pitch go by. The umpire called a ball. The batter let out a huge sigh and looked up at the sky. He had survived to swing one more time. The count: one ball, two strikes. If all went right for the Asahi, the next pitch could really tighten the noose.

Reggie was asking for the same pitch, low and outside. Teddy nodded briefly. Winding up, told himself to believe in the possibility, and threw as hard as he could. The pitch curved to the outside and dropped. This time the lanky batter was ready to get a piece of the ball.

Just like Teddy and the defense had hoped, the batter hit toward third, but the ball was a slow roller. Roy Yamamura, substituting for Teddy at shortstop, ran full tilt to pick up the ball. Known as the "Dancing Shortstop" because of his athleticism, Roy never wasted motion while he was catching or throwing, and it was a joy to watch how fluid he could be.

Roy threw to second, and Frank Nakamura caught the ball and wheeled to throw to first. His toss was high and hard, and looked like it might be out of reach.

But first baseman Charlie Tanaka—the tallest player in the club's history and apparently born to play first base—stretched his long, thin frame as far as humanly possible and gathered the ball in. At almost the same time, the batter stepped on first base.

The white first-base umpire had no doubts. "Out!"

The taut, heavy mood at the Powell Street Grounds disappeared momentarily. There was applause for the fine double play, but the atmosphere soon grew tense again.

Play resumed with two outs and a runner still on third. The fifth batter, who'd hit the come-from-behind home run in the bottom of the fourth, was up again. Naturally, BC hoped for another home run, and the team's fans were in an uproar. Meanwhile, the Asahi fans were praying.

To Teddy, this was a revenge match. There was no vacillation. His first pitch was high and outside. The batter took a mighty swing that made the crowd go oooooh, but missed. Teddy had pitched the ball the batter wanted and beaten him.

The second and third pitches also tempted the batter to swing, but he kept his bat on his shoulder. The count: two balls, one strike. If this guy makes it on base, he could score the come-from-behind run. Teddy couldn't afford to throw any more intentional balls.

Reggie trotted to the mound. "Your straight fastball is a good pitch," he said. "It's dangerous, but let's go for it. Even if he gets a hit, the score would be even." That was exactly what Teddy was thinking.

Play resumed. The crowd was making an incredible amount of noise. Within the whirlwind of sound, Teddy calmly wound up. He was aiming for the first championship. Just believe in the pitch and throw with no regrets. He released the ball, the pitch going outside and low. His will proved stronger than the batter's, who seemed to swing and miss in slow motion. The count was now two and two.

Reggie nodded his head. Okay, we've got this.

Teddy's fifth pitch flew straight and high toward the edge of the strike zone. The batter knew what was coming, seeing the ball seem to float up, and swung hard.

Instead of the thunderous crack of bat on ball, there was a dry thump as the ball hit Reggie's mitt. The crowd stared as the batter lost his balance and fell to the ground.

"Strike! You're out!"

At the umpire's call, Reggie ran to Teddy on the mound with the ball in his mitt.

"Banzai, banzai!"

A roar that had never been heard before enveloped the Powell Street Grounds. Nikkei fans streamed onto the field to celebrate with their heroes.

A ring of people surrounded the mound. Harry Miyasaki was thrown upward once, twice. The hands of the team and fans sent captain Tom Matoba and then winning pitcher Teddy Furumoto high into the air as well.

The Asahi and their fans were in tears. Some were red-faced with excitement. When the pandemonium had died down a little, they could hear applause and cheers for the Asahi from supporters of the BC team.

The Asahi had fought with Nikkei pride against one of the best white teams and won. They held the championship in their hands, achieving the goal set thirteen years ago when the team was formed.

As for Harry Miyasaki, the manager who had led the Asahi to the Terminal League title, one sportswriter for a Vancouver daily said: "He's the Japanese John McGraw."

John McGraw, of course, was the manager of the legendary New York Giants. As his nickname "Little Napoleon" implied, McGraw was a rare strategist and tactician who had engineered the Giants' golden age. For a white journalist to compare Harry to this famous baseball skipper—who remains a giant in the annals of

Major League history—was astounding.

The exhilaration of their first league pennant continued to resonate throughout Japan Town. It is said that the exhilaration was more intense than if the team had won the World Series. Their victory was not confined to the sport of baseball, either. To the Nikkei, it was thrilling validation of their worth in Canadian sports history, and an unforgettable event in the lives of everyone of Japanese descent living and striving in Canada.

The Vancouver All-Star team that barnstormed through Japan in 1921.
Back row, from left: Joe Niimi, Teddy Furumoto, Harry Yoshioka, Arni Papuki, team leader
Seitaro Nomura, Yuji Uchiyama, unidentified, Mickey Kitagawa, Tom Miyata
Front row, from left: Yu Nishizaki, Yoshi Oka, unidentified, unidentified, Yo Horii,
Eddy Kitagawa, Joe Brown

The considerably expanded Asahi team, ca. 1923

Back row, from left: Roy Yamamura, Frank Nakamura, unidentified, Reggie Yasui,
unidentified, unidentified, Teddy Furumoto, Harry Miyasaki, M. Sato, G. Kato,
Eddy Kitagawa, S. Nakamura, B. Higuchi, C. Hayashi, J. Nishimura, T. Suga

Middle row, from left: T. Yamamoto, unidentified, B. Sekine, unidentified, G. Aoki,
S. Miyasaki, T. Kurita, T. Kuzuhara (team doctor), K. Shiomi, R. Kawasaki,
unidentified, S. Miki, unidentified, B. Okada, K. Mizuno, F. Nishikawa, J. Sekine

Front row, from left: H. Shibuya, J. Fukui, A. Korenaga, Mickey Maikawa, G. Ishiwara,
F. Miyazaki (five years old), G. Nishimura, T. Kuzuhara (five years old), K. Kutsutake,
T. Hori, I. Ebata, Y. Korenaga, M. Imada, T. Naruse, H. Inoue

The Giants and a Dream Come True

Harry Miyasaki did his best to keep strengthening the Asahi. He wanted to make the team an invincible force. He recruited players from other Nikkei teams, and on occasion would even persuade an white player to join the club.

Being a manager and a full-time business owner was taxing, though, and at the end of the 1929 season Harry resigned to concentrate on the family laundry and dry cleaning businesses.

However the foundation he created over eight years with the team would not crumble so easily. In 1930, and again in 1933, the Asahi were champions of the Terminal League. In the Pacific Northwest League, made up of Nikkei teams, the Asahi were overwhelmingly victorious time after time.

After Tom Matoba retired at the end of the 1930 season, none of the original members of the Asahi remained. However, the depth of the team that Harry had built up so carefully was undeniable. The Asahi's position as the most popular team in Vancouver, with the greatest crowds, had also been firmly established.

In 1935, the Asahi played against the Dai-Nichi Tokyo Baseball Club, the predecessors of the Yomiuri Giants.

The U.S. Major League All-Stars, which included Babe Ruth and Lou Gehrig, had played exhibition matches in Japan in the autumn of 1934. The Dai-Nichi Tokyo Baseball Club was the all-star Japanese team created for those exhibition games, and went on to become Japan's first professional team.

The first Japanese professional baseball league, comprised of seven teams, would not be established until the following year. In the meantime, there was no one for the Dai-Nichi squad to play, so they embarked on a long barnstorming tour to Mexico and North America.

It was eventually decided that the team name, the Dai-Nippon Tokyo Baseball Club, was much too long. They became known as the Tokyo Kyojin, and later as the Tokyo Giants.

During their 1935 exhibition tour, the Tokyo Kyojin played against minor-league teams. In America and Canada, the majority of their games were against Nikkei teams, including the Asahi.

The Tokyo Kyojin pitcher Eiji Sawamura was famous among the Nikkei and other baseball fans in Canada and the United States. When the major leaguers had toured Japan the previous year, Sawamura had struck out their sluggers and allowed only one hit. The Asahi team worshipped Sawamura, as well as Victor Starfin, nicknamed the "Russian Rocket," and Tokyo Big Six University star Shigeharu Mizuhara. It was a dream come true for the Vancouver Asahi to play against the Tokyo Kyojin.

Their two games against the Kyojin, on May 18 and 24, were played in Con Jones Stadium in Vancouver. The lineups for both teams—in batting order, with defensive positions in parentheses—for the first game were as follows:

Vancouver Asahi
Frank Shiraishi (LF), Roy Yamamura (2B), Mike Maruno (SS), Reggie Yasui (C), Herbie Tanaka (3B), Mauji Masuda (RF), Joe Fukui (1B), Abe Korenaga (CF), Kaz Suga (P)

Tokyo Kyojin
Takeo Tanabe (SS), Kumeyasu Yajima (L), Usaburo Shintomi (R), Fumihito Hori (CF), Fujio Nagasawa (1B), Shigeru Mizuhara (3B), Yukio Eguchi (2B), Tamotsu Uchibori (C), Kenichi Aoshiba (P), Victor Starfin (P)

The Kyojin won that game 8-3. The Asahi were able to score just one run in the second game, and again went down in defeat.

Mickey Maikawa, who had retired from the Asahi a year earlier, was there for the games. "The Tokyo Kyojin were awesome in batting and defense," he recalled. "It was like watching a game between professionals and amateurs."

Regrettably, Eiji Sawamura did not step on the mound for either game, but he did participate in practices and pitched to the Asahi players. An "old boy" of the Asahi team testified, "It wasn't easy to hit Sawamura's pitches because he was so fast."

The Asahi failed to show their teeth in the face of the Japanese All-Stars. Conversely, the Kyojin felt they should not take the Asahi lightly. The Asahi's popularity was even greater than they had heard in Japan.

The Kyojin were able to cover much of the cost of the barn-storming tour from the box-office receipts. It was one thing when playing against Nikkei teams, but the turnout for games against white teams was very low. This state of affairs had a negative affect on meals for the players.

In Canada, however, massive crowds gathered for games in Edmonton and Winnipeg, where the Kyojin played in addition to Vancouver. Whether they played a Nikkei team or a white team, Nikkei fans came, and a good number of white spectators were attendees as well. This was a direct result of the immense popularity of the Asahi, who drew both Nikkei and white fans.

Both games between the Asahi and the Kyojin attracted huge audiences. The Nikkei spectators cheered for the Kyojin, happy to have the chance to encourage a team that had come all the way from Japan, but the white fans considered the Asahi their home team, and cheered them on.

"Go Asahi!"

"Go Yamamura!"

The Tokyo Kyojin were renamed the Tokyo Giants after return-ing to Japan. They came back for a second North American tour in 1936, the following year. They immediately concluded a contract with the Vancouver Asahi for games during the second tour, realizing that this would attract the greatest number of spectators.

## The Last Championship

The Asahi, the Nikkei ball team of choice, were now famous among baseball fans throughout Canada. The team regularly received invitations for games, including calls from many white teams in the United States, which boosted the number of road games and travel time.

Spectators at some of the away games, depending upon the location, had never seen a Nikkei baseball team before. The crowds would watch intently as the Asahi practiced.

What they noticed was that the players were physically smaller but moved quickly and relentlessly on defense and offense without seeming to tire. The Asahi also made plays that constantly surprised the watching crowds, and their popularity continued to rise.

Winning in the Terminal League became a matter of routine. The Asahi looked for a chance to step up. Based on the team's standing in the Terminal League, the Senior City League extended an invitation to join. Unlike the Terminal League, this league was not strictly amateur. It included professional and semi-professional players, and cash would be handed out to the Asahi players as dinner money after every game.

There was no reason for the Vancouver Asahi to refuse the invitation. They moved to a new venue within the city, Athletic Park, to continue their challenge.

From time to time, the league sponsors would organize a special team by recruiting only professional and semipro players to play against the Vancouver Asahi. Despite the increase in the Asahi's white fanbase, the storm of discrimination still raged one step outside the protective confines of Japan Town. It was also a fact that the numbers of white spectators would dramatically increase if a team defeated the popular Nikkei team. There was a good deal of speculation over the team performances.

It was a different Vancouver Asahi that faced the pros and semi-pros. This is not to say that the Asahi could not handle a higher level of play. It was disappointing for all the fans with high expectations, however, when the Asahi could only come up with average results. The Asahi withdrew from the Senior City League in 1936.

Although the Asahi's advance to the Senior City League had fallen through, it was not a serious setback for the team. They quickly regrouped and moved forward.

The Asahi were amateur baseball players to the end. They just loved to play baseball, and wanted to test themselves against strong teams. They did not play baseball for money, nor did they regard it as work. It was their love for the game that captured the hearts of their fans, and the purity of the sport that created a legend.

The Great Depression that had gripped the United States in 1929 had global repercussions. Canada also endured a long and difficult economic downturn. All of the Asahi players were in desperate need of work just to keep food on the table. After working long hours, the players would wolf down a few bites and then head to the playing field. That was their daily routine.

The environment for professional baseball players and for the Vancouver Asahi team was totally different, and the difference made it impossible to exploit the Asahi players' full potential.

Some players on the Vancouver Asahi had skills on a par with the pros and had been invited to big-league tryouts in the United States. "If only he could play in the Major Leagues," fans fantasized about more than a few players. But no one in the Vancouver Asahi ever played as a professional athlete. It was more important, and more of an honor, to play for the Vancouver Asahi.

Through it all, the Japanese community never wavered in their passionate support, nor did they yield their ardent expectations for the Vancouver Asahi. They welcomed the club back to their old Powell Street home field.

The great coach and manager Harry Miyasaki himself, stealing time from his busy schedule, would come to look after the Vancouver Asahi as an advisor. His passion for promoting Nikkei baseball had not diminished even after his retirement as a player, coach and manager. In his zeal, he would often have the Asahi show off their play in front of other Nikkei teams.

After withdrawing from the Senior League, and with their fans backing them, the team gathered their strength to build their golden age. In 1938, the Vancouver Asahi conquered the Burrard, Commercial, and Pacific Northwest Japanese leagues, becoming a triple champion. Moreover, they took consecutive Pacific Northwest League championships (1937 and 1938), and went on to win three consecutive championships in the Burrard League (1938, 1939, 1940). In essence, the Vancouver Asahi swept all of the top-ranked amateur leagues in the Northwest.

Coverage of the Vancouver Asahi enlivened local newspapers, both English and Japanese, every day during the season. The number of both white and Japanese spectators visiting the stadium to watch the team rose. Race did not seem to matter anymore. Fans surrounded the team wherever they went.

In terms of the Nikkei kids and young women hotly pursuing autographs and sometimes more, the Vancouver Asahi players were more popular than any modern idol or superstar. Praised by the Issei (first generation) as the "pride of the Japanese Canadians," the players were, in their adoring fans' eyes, beings closer to gods. The team was even regarded with awe by white fans and players.

Summer's end, 1941. The Vancouver Asahi players were ecstatic about their latest victory in the Pacific Northwest League, which featured Nikkei teams from both the United States and Canada.

The team had won a total of eight Pacific Northwest championships, five of them consecutively. They had shown themselves to
be head and shoulders above the rest of the clubs, and were shoot-
ing for a sixth consecutive championship in 1942. Both players and
fans looked forward to not just another Pacific Northwest League
title, but also to victories in other league tournaments against
veteran white teams. The Asahi were on a roll, and it looked as if
nothing could stop them.

At the time, no one could have imagined that this would be the
last championship ever for the Vancouver Asahi.

**CHAPTER 6**

# A Tragedy Unfolds

## "Jap Planes Attack Pearl Harbor"

About three months had passed since the Asahi won their fifth straight Pacific Northwest League title. With invitational games, exhibitions and their regular practice schedule, the team was still steeped in baseball every day during the off-season.

Unusually for the rainy season, a crisp and clear winter morning dawned in Vancouver on the morning of December 7, 1941. The church bells announcing services had resonated in the calm, and the time was about half past nine.

A news announcement suddenly interrupted an entertainment program on the radio. Japan Town was wrapped in stunned silence at the news. The Japanese armed forces had attacked Pearl Harbor that morning.

The Nikkei community had been worried about the gradually deteriorating relations between Japan and America. But no one could believe that Japan would suddenly attack the United States.

It must be some kind of mistake, they thought.

Those people who did not own a radio, and who had heard the news by word of mouth, were confused and frightened. They tried to confirm what had happened by calling the newspaper offices and by asking other Nikkei.

The radio continued to broadcast war news bulletins. It was broadcast that Japanese forces had simultaneously invaded the Malay Peninsula and Manila in the Philippines. Japan had declared war on the United States and Great Britain. The radio aired emergency orders for Canadian soldiers on leave to return immediately to their units.

There was no room left for doubt: Japanese armed forces had attacked Pearl Harbor.

What was done was done, and some among the Issei, whose bonds to their homeland were strong, said, "They did it, Japan actually did it!" They were surprised but not unhappy when they heard about the success of Japan's attack on Pearl Harbor. They did not doubt that the war would be over quickly, with Japan victorious.

But Japan declaring war on the United Kingdom meant that Japan and Canada, a member of the British Commonwealth, were also at war. The Japanese immigrants and their descendants already faced discrimination and rejection on a daily basis. What would happen now? Uneasiness and fear clutched at the Nikkei's hearts. And many wondered, as the days passed, if they would be allowed to play their favorite pastime as freely as before.

Without making a distinction between first-generation immigrants, second-generation Nikkei born and raised in Canada and naturalized citizens, the Canadian government declared all Japanese Canadians as local enemy aliens.

Forty Japanese community leaders were arrested, classified as dangerous persons. Japanese schools were ordered closed. Fishing and sailing were banned. Japanese newspapers were ordered to stop the presses. Speaking in Japanese on the telephone—and even making long-distance calls—was prohibited.

The attack on Pearl Harbor brought a terrible retaliation that went far beyond the fears and trepidations of the Nikkei.

## The End of Japan Town

The year following the outbreak of war, the Canadian government took steps that effectively destroyed the foundations of Nikkei society, all in the name of wartime defense.

To defend the country against Japanese attack, an area one hundred miles wide along the Pacific coastline was created. No Nikkei were allowed within this quarantine area.

All boys and men between the ages of 18 and 45 were sent to the mountain camps, ostensibly to work on highway construction. Those who resisted or objected were sent to prison camps. Japanese-Canadian families were sent to camps east of the Rockies, and to Ontario, Manitoba, and Alberta to work the sugar beet fields. Everyone of Japanese ancestry in British Columbia was forcibly relocated to inland provinces in eastern Canada.

Nikkei living in Vancouver and Steveston were forcibly moved directly from their homes to their destinations. However, Nikkei who lived outside of these two areas were first assembled in Vancouver's Hastings Park. All Japanese were required to leave within 24 hours after being served eviction notices. Hastings Park began to fill up.

The only preparations made for the Nikkei were hastily converted animal stalls from the Pacific National Exhibition in Hastings Park. The stench of the stalls was terrible, and there was no protection from the wind and rain. They were unfit for human habitation.

Each person was allowed to bring 20 pounds of personal effects, with a total limit of 750 pounds per family. All other property was forfeited. It was promised that government administrators would responsibly manage their possessions and property, but everything left behind by Japanese Canadians, from land to clothing, was auctioned off for next to nothing. Fees for realtors and various sales fees were subtracted. Japanese internees were also required to pay their living expenses, which were also subtracted from the sales price. In short, this was nothing but confiscation of property.

About 22,000 people of Japanese ancestry lived in British Columbia at that time. Other than a few permitted exceptions, such as families working the sugar beet fields in the inland eastern provinces, the majority of Nikkei were moved to isolated camps in the Rockies, such as Kaslo, New Denver, Slocan and Tashme.

The concept of local enemy alien meant that German Canadians and Italian Canadians should have been treated exactly the same as the Japanese Canadians. Although the German and Italian immigrants did suffer hardship, and many were interned in Camp Petawawa, the wholesale eviction and internment the Nikkei suffered was unprecedented. It was overt racial discrimination.

For the Vancouver Asahi, a baseball powerhouse with five straight victories in the Pacific Northwest League and other titles, fate had changed everything. There would be no next season. At a moment's notice, they were going to be living in separate camps, working on roads, and isolated from each other.

Surely, the players thought, Nikkei will be allowed back in Vancouver again in the not-so-distant future.

The evening before leaving Japan Town, they all placed something precious in the one Boston bag that would store everything they were allowed to take to their new destination.

Along with memories, the bags held the hopes and prayers that they would be able to play baseball again to their heart's content.

What was placed so reverently inside was a uniform with a big red "A" on the chest, with an embroidered chrysanthemum crest of the Japanese nobility on the left shoulder.

But the Vancouver Asahi would never again all gather in one place. The team was gone.

## Baseball Inside the Walls

Life in the internment camps was restrictive, crowded, uncomfortable and inconvenient in all respects. The camps of Kaslo, New Denver, Slocan and Tashme were the harshest, located in the Canadian interior where it could drop to minus 30 degrees or lower during the winter. The wooden huts could not keep out the cold. The older men and young boys working on the roads in these camps were able to rejoin their families, however—a small and happy relief.

Entertainment played a big role in camp life, precisely because of all the proscriptions placed on daily life. People were active in club and activity circles. Needless to say, it was baseball that everyone in the camps looked forward to the most.

The first thing the men did in camp was to find a place to play ball. They would look for the best available vacant patch of land and start making a baseball field, organize teams, and the games would begin.

People gathered from every corner of these camps to cheer at games. There was even a camp where a wooden trophy was handcrafted to confer on the league champion.

Inside the camps, whether in the snowy depths of winter or the scorching midsummer, the Japanese played baseball. The game eased their lives and helped to unite them. All of the Asahi players played baseball wherever they were sent. Just as they had been before the war, in the camps they were stars. Ken Kusutake, Mike Maruno, Frank Shiraishi, George Shishido, Kaz Suga and Roy Yamamura were all active players when war broke out, and there was no one who did not know of them and admire them.

Each of these guys shone like gold on the camp teams they joined. As soon as they grasped a bat and a ball, their passion for the game made their blood sing. They were as serious in their play on a newly carved-out camp field as they would be in the grandest league venue.

In the small mountain towns near the camps, there were many white people who had never seen a Japanese person. The towns-people were nervous and fearful of the interned Nikkei.

Among the camp guards, however, there were men who knew of the Vancouver Asahi and the players. Some of them, after discovering there was an Asahi player in the camp near their town, would ask the player for a game.

"To play against a team with an Asahi player would be a real honor. It'll help relations between the Nikkei and the town, too. Will you do it?"

Hostility caused by war, discrimination produced by racial differences. To the interned Japanese, this was an unprecedented opportunity to breathe fresh, free air. The town was persuaded to create a team, and soon league games began between camp and town teams. It took time, but little by little, high up in the isolated mountains near ghost towns, something was born between the players, the teams, the interned, and the towns. Mutual understanding began to grow. Some white residents even expressed sympathy at the hardships the internees were suffering.

"Why are they treated like this just because they're Japanese?" the people in town began to ask.

Even if only by small increments, baseball had the power to neutralize hate.

**CHAPTER 7**

# An End to Suffering

## Make Your Choice: Forced Migration or Deportation

Life under compulsory expropriation was painfully restrictive and caused great psychological distress. The Nikkei were torn between loyalty to Canada and to their homeland of Japan. There was also conflict and a growing gap between the Issei, with their deep and complex emotional ties to Japan, and the second-generation Nisei, born and raised in Canada.

Why must we fight in the camps about our identity? Aren't we all Japanese Canadian? How long will this continue? We want to go home as soon as the war ends. We want to go back to our lives before the war.

All such hopes the Nikkei held were shattered. The end of the war only meant the beginning of new trials.

The Canadian government feared the revival of prewar Japanese society, and would not permit a return to their old life. The government gave the Nikkei a choice: Either agree to move to a location in

Canada east of the Rocky Mountains or be deported back to Japan. In short, all Nikkei were to be expelled from British Columbia, where the greatest immigrant foothold had existed.

Close to half of the Nikkei, about ten thousand people, felt fearful and insecure about remaining in Canada after being branded as enemy aliens. They elected to return to Japan at first, but the number of would-be returnees decreased dramatically after it became obvious that Japan was suffering the fate of the losing side in a war, including terrible food shortages. In the end, just under three thousand people returned to Japan.

The majority of the Asahi team remained in Canada. Only a small number of players had returned to Japan, some just before the war began, and some in the immediate postwar period.

It was only after March 31, 1949, nearly three and a half years after the war, that citizenship was restored to the Nikkei, and permission to return to British Columbia was granted.

Since all of the Nikkei properties and possessions left behind had been confiscated and sold, however, there was nothing to return to. The Canadian government was cautious about the revival of a concentrated Japanese community, and discouraged any moves to a single area.

Thus, the greater part of the Nikkei settled in eastern Canada, where they had been forced to migrate. Only a daring few returned to British Columbia. The Nikkei began efforts to integrate with white society. The insular world of Japanese society, which had brought wariness and hostility from whites, effectively disappeared.

During World War II, Japanese immigrants were also labeled enemy aliens in the United States and Brazil. In both countries, Japanese were forced into camps and their properties seized and sold. However, Canada was the only country that prohibited the Nikkei from returning to their hometowns, as well as continuing to deprive them of citizenship despite the war having ended.

The start of the war began the disintegration of Japan Town. After the war, no Japanese community in Canada ever grew to a level that could be called a Japan Town or Little Tokyo, making it virtually impossible for a Nikkei team like the Vancouver Asahi to rise again.

The Vancouver Asahi had shouldered the pride of the Nikkei, the mission to challenge established teams, and to become undisputed champions. The Asahi quietly put away their proud history as the Nikkei began their efforts to reassimilate into Canadian society.

Although the Japanese community in Vancouver had collapsed and the Asahi had dissolved, there was something that could never disappear, and continued to grow among the former players: their pure passion for baseball. Perhaps it is appropriate to call these players "crazy for baseball," since as long as there was time they never tired of chasing that white, horsehide-covered ball.

Even when all their property was seized, their citizenship revoked, and they were driven from the city where they lived, the Asahi players never thought to abandon baseball. In the intense heat and numbing cold of the camps, they played for their future. That did not change even when they were forbidden to go home and forced to live in eastern Canada after the war.

Along with the other Nikkei, the Asahi players moved east and settled in the big cities of Toronto and Montreal. Once people found out there were former Vancouver Asahi members living in town, local teams aggressively recruited them. Though once considered "enemy aliens," they also got invitations to play from other minority clubs and white teams. Nothing could have made the Asahi players happier.

The level of play of the ex-Asahi members was much higher than the other amateur baseball teams. Some of Asahi players like Ken Suga wandered from team to team, helping them to triumph. Other players stuck with one team, leading them to higher standings.

Ex-Asahi players too old to play became coaches and officials, passing on the detail-oriented strategies and work ethic of their vaunted team.

The Asahi's last shortstop, Roy Yamamura, was a typical Asahi "old boy" who contributed to Canadian regional baseball development. The wonderfully nicknamed "Dancing Shortstop," beloved by both Nikkei and white fans, devoted his later years to volunteering as a Little League umpire. He became known as "Mr. Umpire," and was praised for his long commitment to the game's betterment.

Although the Vancouver Asahi never revived, the passion of its former players kept the soul of the team alive on Canada's ball fields long after the war that had broken them apart.

## Redress Settlement Victory

Canada's Japanese residents, who suffered as victims of the Canadian government's severe policies of forced migration, began to rebuild their lives. Thirty years after the war and enduring and overcoming much hardship, life could finally be considered stable again.

It was just about that time, in 1977, that the Canadian government certified Manzou Nagano as the first official Japanese immigrant. The centennial of Japanese immigration was also celebrated. The anniversary events presented a variety of festive entertainment and an exhibition that highlighted historical records, photographs and memorabilia of the past century. This exhibition became the trigger for change for the country's citizens of Japanese heritage.

As the exhibition traveled to various cities around Canada, many Nikkei were determined to raise questions about the Canadian government's unjustified actions, both during and after the war.

At the beginning of the 1980s, the U.S. Congress had investigated the treatment of Japanese Americans during World War II, specifically on how property was illegally seized and people incarcerated in camps. Congress concluded that the U.S. government had committed a gross violation of human rights, and recommended that a formal apology and compensation be rendered to Japanese Americans.

Influenced by what was happening south of the border, a similar movement to request redress (correction and compensation for injustice) for the suffering incurred by unjustified measures by the Canadian government began.

In the United States, apology and compensation issues were influenced in part by the political stance of the federal government and Congress, which valued strengthening relations with Japan. In Canada, however, the redress movement originated with and was pushed forward by Japanese Canadians.

Central to the redress movement were the Sansei, or third-generation Japanese Canadians. Among the Nikkei, it is said that "the Issei (first generation) endured; the Nisei (second generation) survived." In other words, the Issei and Nisei lived through the reality of unfair treatment by the government. It was up to the Sansei to formally object to the wrongs done, and demand redress.

The parents of the Sansei worked to reconstruct their lives after the war, and to provide the best education possible to ensure their children a better future. The Sansei, many of whom became lawyers, politicians and successful professionals with social standing and influence, organized the redress movement.

It was not easy. Negotiations with the Canadian government regarding redress were extremely difficult. In the meantime, differences of opinion within the Nikkei community caused discord. The redress movement followed many twists and turns.

The Sansei presented the redress movement as a matter central to Canadian democracy. In this way they were able to gain across-the-board support from all Canadian minority groups. The victory of the redress movement was in part made possible thanks to Canada's basic policy of advocating multiculturalism.

After four long years of negotiations, Prime Minister Brian Mulroney and representatives of the National Association of Japanese Canadians signed an agreement on September 22, 1988. Redress for the discriminatory actions by the Canadian government during and after the war was promised at last. Just one month to the day earlier, the U.S. government had formally announced that Japanese Americans would receive compensation.

The success of the powerful redress movement recovered honor for the Nikkei. This power would also revive the proud legend of the Vancouver Asahi, who had challenged and won against the best and strongest of Canada's baseball teams.

Powell Street in the late 1990s.

Author Ted Y. Furumoto at the site where the Powell Baseball Grounds used to be in the 1990s. Now it's called Oppenheimer Park.

**EPILOGUE**

# Sixty-Two Years Later

### Induction into the Hall of Fame

On February 24, 2003, a little less than a year after members of the Vancouver Asahi were invited to throw the first pitch at Toronto's Sky Dome, more good news reached them: the Canadian Baseball Hall of Fame had decided to induct the team.

To be inducted into the Hall of Fame is the greatest honor for anyone connected with baseball. There are similar baseball halls of fame in the United States and Japan, filled with players, managers and coaches who have made remarkable achievements or contributed to the development of the game.

The induction ceremony was scheduled for June 28, four months later, and would be held at the Canadian Baseball Hall of Fame, located in St. Mary's, Ontario.

As the master of ceremonies announced "The Vancouver Asahi!" and began to call out the names of the players, the two hundred people in attendance rose to give the team a thunderous standing ovation. The four players able to attend this pre-induction event—Mickey Maikawa, Ken Kusutake, Kiyoshi Suga and Kaye Kaminishi—seemed puzzled at first by the applause and cheers, but soon had tears in their eyes.

With the addition of Mike Maruno, five players from the Asahi team took part in the induction ceremony the next day.

Richard Belec, who had worked to develop Canada's local teams and leagues, was also honored, as were former major leaguers Joe Carter and Kirk McCaskill. Joe Carter, who had played for the Toronto Blue Jays, was by far the biggest draw.

The Asahi players, all in their eighties and nineties now, stood beaming on the stage. Standing with them was Tom Valcke, president and CEO of the Hall of Fame. He began with the following words: "We have to repay a debt …"

Respect was paid to the pride of the Nikkei, the Vancouver Asahi, who had charmed fans and opposing white teams with formidable talent and pure sportsmanship. The Asahi were inducted not only because of their ability but also as a heartfelt gesture of acknowledgement of and compensation for the injustices they suffered.

A strong thread that cannot be severed connects the Asahi to the victory of the redress movement, the Canadian Baseball Hall of Fame, and the Sky Dome ceremony. If Canada had not recognized the need for redress, the legend of the Vancouver Asahi might never have been revived and recognized. The Asahi would have just faded from postwar memories.

From inception to dissolution, approximately seventy players had belonged to the Vancouver Asahi, and many more had played for their farm teams. The players still alive at the time of the induction ceremony numbered eight. After prolonged applause and cheers, the five Asahi players there donned their commemorative jackets. Ken Kusutake, representing the team, thanked the Hall of Fame.

"On behalf of all the members, past and present, it is with great pride and gratitude that we accept this honor. All those who have gone on to their field of dreams must be looking down on us with feelings of pride and happiness and the satisfaction of a job well done."

After Kusutake's speech, the other "old boys" read out the complete list of Asahi players. "This honor was given to everyone who played for the Vancouver Asahi," he emphasized.

The ceremony came to a climax with the induction of the Vancouver Asahi. The next day, the Ontario newspaper announced, "ASAHI VICTORY YESTERDAY." The Vancouver newspapers, which had been dark with anti-Japanese sentiment before the war, also happily headlined the news of the induction.

Sixty-two years after its untimely dissolution, the team was no longer just a Nikkei legend. With their entry into the Hall of Fame, the Vancouver Asahi became a bona fide Canadian legend.